The Christian Universe

THE BOYLE LECTURES 1965

The Christian Universe

E. L. MASCALL

*Professor of Historical Theology in the
University of London*

Darton, Longman & Todd

First published in Great Britain in 1966 by
Darton, Longman & Todd Ltd
Reprinted 1967
64 Chiswick High Road, London W4
© 1966 Dr E. L. Mascall
Printed in Great Britain by
The Bowering Press, Plymouth

Acknowledgments

The author and publishers acknowledge with thanks the permission of the copyright-holders for the use of passages from the following works:

To Messrs Burns & Oates Ltd, for an extract from *St John of the Cross* by E. Allison Peers and from *Science, Religion and Christianity* by H. U. von Balthasar; to Messrs William Collins Sons & Co. Ltd, for an extract from *Le Milieu Divin* by P. Teilhard de Chardin; to Messrs Doubleday & Co. Inc., for an extract, "The Lesson of the Moth", from *Archy and Mehitabel* by Don Marquis; to Messrs David Higham Associates Ltd, for an extract from *Paradiso* by Dante translated by Barbara Reynolds; to Messrs John Murray Ltd, for an extract from "Christmas" from *Collected Poems* by John Betjeman; to Miss D. E. Collins and Messrs A. P. Watt & Son for an extract from *The Higher Unity* by G. K. Chesterton.

Contents

Foreword

Apart from a few minor modifications, these lectures are printed in the form in which they were prepared to be delivered in the Church of St. James, Piccadilly, by kind permission of the Rector, The Reverend John Brewis, in October and November 1965. The conversational style has been retained.

CHAPTER ONE

World without God

WHEN THE HONOURABLE ROBERT BOYLE DIED IN THE year 1691, he established, by his will, a course of eight sermons to be delivered, as he said, "for ever, or at least for a considerable number of years" by "some learned Divine or Preaching Minister resident within the City of London, or extent of the Bills of Mortality", an area later extended to the Administrative County of London. These sermons, or lectures, were to be "for proving the Christian Religion against notorious Infidels, namely Atheists, Theists, Pagans, Jews and Mahometans, not descending lower to any controversies that are among Christians themselves", and they were to be "assisting to all Companies and encouraging them in any undertakings for propagating the Christian Religion in Foreign parts, To be ready to satisfy such real scruples as any might have concerning those matters, and to answer such new objections or difficulties as might be started, to which good answers had not been made." This seemed in itself to be a sufficiently daunting assignment, but I must admit that, when the Lord Bishop of London honoured me with the invitation to deliver the Boyle Lectures for this year, my chief misgiving was concerned with the inclusion of Theism as one of the notorious infidelities which I was commissioned to demolish, since I had always understood the word "theism" to signify, in the words of the Oxford English Dictionary, "belief in a deity or deities, as opposed to *atheism*" or "belief in one God, as opposed to *polytheism* or *pantheism*". For a moment I wondered whether the pious founder had been granted a prophetic insight into the demands of some of the more radical Christian thinkers of the present day, and I wondered, too, whether I should have to fall back upon the second meaning of the word "theism", which connotes – I quote the Oxford Dictionary again – "a morbid condition characterised by headache, sleeplessness, and palpitation of the heart, caused by excessive tea-drinking". At this point, however, I was fortunate to discover that, at the time when Boyle made his will, the word "theism" was commonly used to mean what we denote at the present day by the rather similar word "deism", namely "belief in the existence of a God, with rejection of revelation"; and I breathed again freely. For I have no desire to reject revelation.

It will, I think, be well to begin by explaining just what it is that, in this course of lectures, I shall be trying to do. To put the matter quite simply, I hope to show that the affirmations about God, man and Christ which the Christian Church has taught throughout its history, and the manner of living which those affirmations imply, are more satisfying to our intellect, more enriching to our imagination and more fulfilling to our whole personality than either the secularist humanism which is so widespread today or the etiolated substitutes for orthodox Christianity which are frequently offered for our consumption. I hope, in short, to show that the Faith which the Church has proclaimed throughout the ages is fuller, more interesting, more comprehensive, more demanding, more liberating, more satisfying, that it synthetises a wider range of human thought, embraces and co-ordinates a wider range of human experience, opens up more possibilities of human living and offers in the end a deeper and richer ecstasy of fulfilment than any alternative way of life and thought; that it is in every way grander, more inspiring and more fruitful. I shall not put before you many arguments, in the narrow sense of that word. There are plenty of books that do that; I have even ventured to write some myself. What I want to do rather, if I can, is to catch your imagination, to help you to see what a magnificent and (to use the word that is so popular today) what an exciting thing this Christianity is. Then, if you are not already a convinced Christian, I hope you will think it worth while to enquire into the truth of the Christian Faith; I cannot expect you to decide about that simply as a result of listening to these lectures. If you are already a convinced Christian, I hope they may perhaps increase your confidence in the Faith and your understanding of it. For we are so incessantly told by people, both outside and inside the Church, that orthodox

Christianity is narrow and sterile that we may find our-selves coming to believe that this is so. I shall try to observe to the best of my ability the instructions of Robert Boyle that the Lecturer must not descend to any controversies that are among Christians themselves. This is, however, no easy task today, if it ever was; even in Boyle's own day I am fairly sure that many of those people whom he called Theists, and whom he ordered the Lecturer to refute, would have claimed that they were themselves Christians, in the truest and deepest sense of the word. So if, in attempting to obey my in-structions, I find myself sometimes sailing rather close to the wind, I hope I shall be forgiven both by Boyle and by his Trustees.

There is one favour, and only one, which I want to ask of my audience; that is that you will not dismiss any of the assertions which I make simply because they appear to be "orthodox" or "traditional". I hope I may pay you the compliment of assuming that what you are concerned with is in the first place truth and in the second place relevance. No theory, outlook or point of view can in the long run be of the slightest use to any of us if it is false. Nothing is, I think, more basically crude and more ultimately stupid than to commend, or to accept, a theory simply because it is "new"; for the one thing that we can be sure of about anything that is new is that before very long it will be old. This does not matter in the case of clothes or even in the case of detergents, for detergents are used up and clothes wear out. We have had at least three "new theologies" in the present century, two in England and one in France. Now there is, of course, a sense in which the theology of one age and place will differ from that of another; people must be spoken to in ways that they can understand and that they can see to be relevant to their concerns. But the hard core of Christian truth is the same for one age and place as for another. Its claim is not to be new, but to be permanent; and, while it has the most wonderful power to address men and women where they stand, it must also sometimes point out to them that they are standing in the wrong place or that the place where they are standing is not where they think it is. To maintain the Faith in its integrity and at the same time to express it in contemporary terms is no easy task, and today it is perhaps more difficult than it has ever been before. But it is precisely in grappling with this task in each age that the Church acquires new understanding of her faith and sees new implications in it. To describe it as "orthodox" is not to imply that it is rigid or sterile, but rather that it is infinitely fertile and adaptable; to say that it is "traditional" is not to say that it is of this or that century, but that it is for all. And we may be sure of this, that a theology which is more concerned to be contemporary than to be true will have neither the right nor the power to influence the contemporary world; all that it can do is to win a grudging and contemptuous toleration by the world, on the condition that, whatever else it does, it does not challenge the world's assumptions about itself. As Dorothy Sayers stringently remarked:

> Our successors will speak of "the Neo-Elizabethans" precisely as we speak of "the Victorians", and in the same tone of voice; "depth-psychology" will take its place in their museums alongside of "faculty-psychology"; "faith in the future" will seem to them as reprehensible as "nostalgia for the past" does to us; and their journalists will use "twentieth century", as ours use "medieval", by way of a handy term for such crudities, cruelties, and superstitions as they may happen to disapprove. We cannot, after all, have it both ways.[1]

In saying, as I shall, that our present age is radically secularised, I mean that, whatever remnants remain in our national life of the trappings of religion – the Remembrance-Day parades, the Magna Carta services, the church weddings and such like – the vast majority of men and women today organise their lives on the assumption that the only realities of which they need to take account are those that are perceived by their senses in the brief span of time that lies between their conception in their mother's womb and their death on the motorway or in the hospital bed. This carries with it two consequences: first, that there is nothing after death that we need bother about, neither heaven, hell nor purgatory; secondly, that there is nothing during

[1] Dante, *The Divine Comedy* (Penguin Classics edition), II, pp. 45f.

this life that we need bother about except the things of this world, neither God nor angels nor devils, neither prayer nor grace nor holiness. There has in fact been a steady corrosion of all the three beliefs which the great eighteenth-century philosopher Immanuel Kant postulated as the foundations of religion: belief in human freedom, in God and in immortality. First, belief in human freedom, which is of course the basis of human responsibility. It would be quite wrong to suppose that scientists in the fields of neurophysiology and cybernetics have shown that human beings, and in particular human brains, are nothing more than elaborate machines; the recent symposium *Minds and Machines*[1] shows how little agreement has been reached about that. It would be equally wrong to suppose that the researches of psychologists have shown that human actions are purely the outcome of factors operating in the subconscious and unconscious regions of the mind; psychologists are far from agreed on this, and even those who are have such conflicting theories as to how this deep-seated determinism operates that they very largely cancel one another out. On the other hand, we must not simply discount or disparage the solid achievements of neurophysiology and psychology; the more we know about our limitations, the more successfully we can plan our actions. Again, it would be unfair and ridiculous to blame the scientists for the steadily rising

[1] Edited by Alan Ross Anderson (1964), Prentice Hall Contemporary Perspectives in Philosophy Series.

crime-rate in our community. It is none the less true that belief in genuine freedom, that is to say belief that we are free to control and direct our actions, has very largely vanished and with it the sense of responsibility; and in its place there has appeared a belief in spurious freedom, that is to say belief that we are morally blameless in following without question, whatever impulses we feel ourselves subject to, on the ground that we are really helpless to do anything else. And clearly, if we are not free to control our own behaviour, we cannot be held responsible for the way in which we behave, either to God or to man. We can neither be blamed for our bad deeds nor praised for our good ones.

The consequences of this may indeed be terrifying; for if we are only machines, we must expect to be used like machines. The suggestion has already been made that before long human beings may be equipped with electrodes in their brains connected to radio-receivers, so that their emotions and their behaviour may be imposed upon them by signals transmitted to them by a scientific élite.[1] (What will happen if the élite find themselves under similar control by a super-élite is an interesting subject for speculation.) I must not, however, follow up these fascinating and horrifying possibilities here. Nor shall I indulge in the elderly pastime of bewailing the delinquency of the young. I merely wish to point to the

[1] Cf. the Report of the CIBA Foundation Conference "Man and his Future", 1963, cited by Arnold Lunn and Garth Lean in *The Cult of Softness*, ch. vi.

very marked loss, in all sections of our community, of the sense of genuine freedom and responsibility; the young are only reaping the wild oats that their parents have sown.

The decay of belief in God is no less obvious, and it would have come as less of a surprise than it has, were it not for the ingrained British habit of taking morality and religion as being not merely closely connected but identical. When we reflect on the barbarities of the Middle Ages, we are inclined to say that people who behaved like that obviously did not really believe in God; and when we observe at the present day the self-sacrificing labours of atheists and agnostics for the welfare of their fellow-men, we are inclined to say that people who behave like this are obviously really unconscious Christians, or believers in disguise. It rarely occurs to us to admit that people may believe in one thing and do another, for we have, as I have already remarked, lost real belief in human freedom. We can no more admit that a sane man's conduct may be inconsistent with his convictions than we can admit that a properly functioning computer can be given a set of data and produce the wrong answer. But I want to plead as strongly as I can that we shall frankly recognise the extent of genuine downright sincere disbelief among our contemporaries today. If we fail to do this, we shall be lacking in respect for their intelligence and integrity, we shall ourselves be hiding our heads in the sand, and we shall adopt a totally wrong strategy for dealing with

B

the situation. Nothing, of course, should prevent us, as believers, from holding that God is in fact at work, so to speak anonymously, even in the minds and lives of those who disbelieve in him; but we must not exasperate them by refusing to take them seriously in their disbelief.

The loss of belief in immortality is equally indisputable, and we are offered every inducement to look upon it as irrelevant or even as a blessing. For scientific technology and welfare-state paternalism have offered us such a dazzling variety of satisfactions, both material and cultural, in this life, that we rarely reflect, except when we cannot avoid it, upon the fact that this life will, for each of us, come to an end. Nevertheless, the fact of death forces itself upon us, and it is very revealing that few of us seem to be able to take it with complete serenity and indifference as simply one – even if the last – of the facts of life. The dog, or even the higher ape, takes it as it comes; clearly there is nothing in his experience that hints that he is made for another life than that of this world. The mature Christian is ready, with St Paul, "to depart and be with Christ", for he knows that this is "much better"[1]. Primitive man is happy to be gathered to his fathers, for he believes that he has fathers to be gathered to. But secularised man, torn as he is between two forces, has to devise various expedients to console himself. On the one hand, he has been conditioned by his secularised environment to think and live as if the sum of human needs and aspirations is limited to this

[1] Philippians i. 23.

world and as if he has neither needs nor resources beyond it. On the other hand, there is his deep-seated instinct – one of the things that distinguishes him from the lower animals – that his ultimate destiny and satisfaction lie elsewhere. What expedients, then, can he devise? The most obvious is to keep his disquiet from rising to the level where it can disturb his emotions, by creating an atmosphere of illusion, by pretending that death does not really occur at all. This is the method of the Californian funeral establishment so brilliantly and ghoulishly depicted by Mr Evelyn Waugh in his novel *The Loved One*; the corpse, skilfully restored to a lifelike appearance by the cosmeticians, is disposed in a natural posture on a *chaise longue* and holds a kind of reception for its friends and relations. A less expensive, and therefore more common, expedient is to put the matter out of one's thoughts and stave off the evil day as long as possible. There is a story about an army recruit who, when he was asked his religion, replied that he was a Methuselahite. To the further enquiry as to the tenets of his sect he answered: "We believe in living as long as possible." The sergeant then not unreasonably asked why in that case he was joining the Army. However, unavowed Methuselahism is, I am sure, the creed of a great many of our contemporaries. Nevertheless sooner or later the fatal day arrives.

> But at my back I always hear
> Time's wingèd chariot hurrying near.

And yonder all before us lie
Deserts of vast eternity.[1]

When the sun sets, it sets to rise again,
But for us, when our brief day is over,
There is one endless night that we must sleep.[2]

For one night or the other night
Will come the Gardener in white,
    And gathered flowers are dead, Yasmin.[3]

A more sophisticated attempt to by-pass the fact of
physical death is provided by those scientific humanists
who make the continuance of the human race a substitute for the survival of the individual. One of the
most notable examples of this is Dr C. H. Waddington,
in his book *The Ethical Animal*, which I have discussed in
detail elsewhere.[4] The plausibility of his argument
almost entirely depends upon his habit of writing about
a personified abstraction called "man". There can of
course be no harm in using the word "man" in a collective sense if we remember that it means just the same as
the plural noun "men". Waddington, however, uses it
as if it denoted some kind of enduring personal being,
who might at one time suffer from privation, disease
and discomfort but whose sufferings could be amply

---

[1] Andrew Marvell, *To his Coy Mistress.*
[2] Catullus, *Carmina*, v.   [3] J. E. Flecker, *Hassan.*
[4] *The Secularisation of Christianity*, pp. 205ff.

compensated for by a prosperous and pleasant existence centuries later. "Man" in the stone age or in nineteenth-century Birmingham or in twentieth-century India may be hungry, sick and wretched, but in the scientific paradise of the twenty-first or twenty-second century he will be couched on the technological equivalent of beds of amarynth and moly. It must be emphasised that these two are simply not the same *man*. There is, of course, a theological sense in which we are all one man in Adam and in Christ, but this is a sense that the scientific humanist would not accept. It is the individual *men* who are born, toil, suffer, rejoice, love, hate and, in the end, die; and no amount of romantic talk about the evolutionary process and the glorious future of the human species – "men like gods" – can get over that fact. Religion has been accused of consoling men for their miseries on earth by promising them pie in the sky when they die; but scientific humanism tries to console them for their present miseries by assuring them that their remote descendents will have plenty of pie on this earth. This is cold comfort. Marxism is more realistic, and its attraction for the newly self-conscious peoples of Asia and Africa rests mainly upon the hope which, however spuriously, it offers, of paradise on earth in our own lifetime. In any case – though this is less relevant – there is no purely scientific ground for assuming that the human race will have an indefinite future. Man has up to now been very lucky, but there is no reason why his luck should go on holding. The nuclear bomb, some uncontrollable virus, a solar flare-up, invasion by organisms from outer space, sheer decline in human fertility, none of these can be ruled out of possibility, nor can we be sure that scientists can defeat them; such confidence is surely not justified by science itself. It is scientific humanists, rather than Christians, who are sometimes guilty of wishful thinking.

Belief in human freedom and responsibility, belief in a transcendent God, belief in human survival of bodily death – these are not the whole of religion, but they are basic elements in historic Christianity, and they have been deep at the roots of the civilisation into which we Europeans have been born. But they are, if not vanished, at any rate very much weakened and corroded today, and we are simply refusing to face the facts if we do not recognise this.

Now the point which I wish to make is this – that, compared with the historic faith of Christendom, the world which is offered to us by modern secularism is restricted, impoverished and quite incapable of satisfying our real needs and aspirations. To show this will not of course suffice to prove that the Christian view is true and the secularist view false. Nevertheless the point must be made, if only for the simple reason that most of our contemporaries have been bamboozled into assuming that the Christian view of the world is so dull and pointless that it is not worth investigating, while the secularist view is liberating and satisfying or at any rate offers solid value for cash down. The reasons for this are complex and mysterious. Most mysterious of all is the fact that many Christians themselves give the impression that their religion is dull and cramping. This is, I think, primarily due to their having themselves become more deeply infected with the circumambient secularist atmosphere than either they or other people recognise. If this is so, the suggestion which we have heard a good deal recently, that the reaction of Christians to secularism should be to make themselves completely secular, would seem to be like trying to cure an alcoholic with larger and larger doses of alcohol. In my second lecture I hope to show that many of our secularists are in fact pretty gloomy in their secularism. But now I want to ask you to consider the wonder and glory of human existence as orthodox Christianity conceives it.

First of all, its splendid range and richness. For secularism, each man's world is limited to that brief span of time that lies between the womb and the tomb and to that limited volume of space and its inhabitants with which he can have dealings in his lifetime. It does, of course, contain many objects worthy of our admiration and many opportunities of experience which are enriching and fulfilling; no Christian should suppose that he is called upon to glorify God by expressing contempt for God's creation. Nevertheless, the world of a man's earthly life is both very limited and extremely fugitive. It is true that many of us are now dazzled by the prospect of travel in space, but we ought not to allow ourselves to be bemused by large distances. We are no doubt right to wonder at the human ingenuity, persistence and courage that has made these things possible, but how much, I wonder, have we succumbed to the vulgar charms of novelty and size? We have, I suggest, just as much, and no more, real cause for admiration of our present-day cosmonauts as an earlier generation had for admiration of the great discoverers of the continent of America and the lands of the Far East. And if we are going to be deluded by figures, at least let us be honestly deluded. One hundred miles above the earth's surface is a very small distance in a universe in which the farthest visible objects are something like two thousand million light-years away (a light year, let us recall, is the distance that light travels in a year with a velocity of about 186,000 miles a second). We talk of "outer space", but it is very much *inner* space in which our cosmonauts travel, if indeed we are to use such pre-Copernican words as "outer" and "inner" at all.

In contrast, the world of human experience as the Christian sees it extends far beyond this earthly life into an infinite future of unending and uncloying bliss, in which, when the last remains of his self-centredness and obstinacy have been consumed, he will be taken up into the life and splendour of God himself. Indeed, even in this life he is offered a foretaste of that supreme glory. And the society which he enjoys, imperfectly here but in its fulness hereafter, is not just that of his earthly contemporaries but that of all the servants of God who have lived upon this earth. Furthermore, he sees this material creation against the vaster and more stupendous background of a realm of pure spirits, and he sees the powers that compose the latter as ranged in a conflict in comparison with which the conflicts on our earthly planet are minute and transient in the extreme. And when he turns his mind again to the material realm of which, so far as his body is concerned, he is part, he sees it as destined not for sheer destruction or unending triviality but for a transformation beyond the wildest speculations of the scientific mind. That is to say, he sees both the material universe and human existence in the light of three great doctrines of the Christian Creed whose full implications he can as yet only begin to grasp – the Communion of Saints, the Resurrection of the Body, and the Life Everlasting. And the guarantee of all this he sees as given in the fact that, in one figure of human history, who was executed in Palestine on a trumped-up charge of sedition when Tiberius was Roman Emperor, the Creator and sustainer of the universe had joined human nature to himself and made it the medium of his own life, and in so doing had raised all human nature to undreamed-of glory and dignity. Thereafter, every man could, in the words of Frederick Rolfe, be "aware of his own unimportant high importance – perfectly conscious of being merely one of quintillions, one (though) for whom the Maker of the Stars had designed to die the atrociously comic death reserved for criminal slaves".[1]

Now if anyone says that he finds this difficult to believe, I shall respect his incredulity, though I shall try to resolve it. But if he says that it is too dull to interest him or too trivial to be worth investigating, I shall be at a loss to imagine what in heaven or earth he would consider to be exciting or important.

May I finish this lecture by reading to you four stanzas from Mr John Betjeman's poem "Christmas":

> And girls in slacks remember Dad,
>   And oafish louts remember Mum,
> And sleepless children's hearts are glad,
>   And Christmas-morning bells say "Come!"
> Even to shining ones who dwell
> Safe in the Dorchester Hotel.
>
> And is it true? And is it true,
>   This most tremendous tale of all,
> Seen in a stained-glass window's hue,
>   A Baby in an ox's stall?
> The Maker of the stars and sea
> Become a Child on earth for me?
>
> And is it true? For if it is,
>   No loving fingers tying strings

---

[1] *The Desire and Pursuit of the Whole,* cit. Cecil Woolf and Brocard Sewell, *New Quests for Corvo,* p. 43.

Around those tissued fripperies,
  The sweet and silly Christmas things,
Bath salts and inexpensive scent
And hideous tie so kindly meant,

No love that in a family dwells,
  No carolling in frosty air,
Nor all the steeple-shaking bells
  Can with this single Truth compare——
That God was Man in Palestine
  And lives today in Bread and Wine.[1]

And is it true? For if it is . . .

[1] *Collected Poems*, pp. 178f.

CHAPTER TWO

Alive with Corpses?

"THE DEAD SEA WAS ALIVE WITH CORPSES."
The author who began a chapter of his book with this
sentence might well have been describing a great deal
of the literature of the present day, and not only crime-
fiction at that. Squalor, frustration, putrescence, downright futility and pointlessness – these are the characteristics of the world and of human life as they are presented to us by many of our novelists and dramatists;
and, although there may be much in this that is
affected, exaggerated, morbid and nasty, it would be a
great mistake if we were to dismiss it as unworthy of
attention. For it witnesses to a conviction that human
life, as it is experienced by many of our contemporaries, is basically unsatisfying and irrational, and this in
spite of the material benefits, increasingly realised and
potentially unlimited, that scientific technology and
the welfare state have made available to us. As Mr
Martin Esslin writes, in his Introduction to the Penguin
Absurd Drama:

There can be no doubt: for many intelligent and sensitive human beings the world of the mid-twentieth
century *has* lost its meaning and has simply ceased to
make sense. Previously held certainties have dis-

solved, the firmest foundations for hope and optimism have collapsed. Suddenly man sees himself faced with a universe that is both frightening and illogical – in a word, absurd. All assurances of hope, all explanations of ultimate meaning have suddenly been unmasked as nonsensical illusions, empty chatter, whistling in the dark.[1]

Mr Richard Kostelanetz has defined "absurd literature" as "works that embody a very specific literary convention: a series of absurd – that is, nonsensical or ridiculous – events that suggest the ultimate absurdity, the ultimate meaninglessness, of human existence".[2] This is a nonsensicality very different in intention and implication from the good-humoured foolery of the verses of Edmund Lear or Lewis Carroll's "Hunting of the Snark". In those we were offered a holiday from the everyday world, in a world which, however fanciful, was, on its own presuppositions, quite remorselessly rational, but here we are presented with meaninglessness at the heart of the everyday world itself. The ultimate meaning of life is that it has no meaning, the innermost shrine of the temple is tenanted by a self-contradiction, the basic law of the universe is expressed by an equation that has no solutions.

Active assertion that the world is meaningless is, of

[1] op. cit., p. 13.
[2] "The American absurd novel", in *The Listener*, 13 May 1965, p. 705.

course, nothing new. It was made twenty years ago in the novels of the French existentialists. M. Sartre's hero Antoine Roquentin was provoked to a disgust amounting to physical nausea by the sight of a chestnut-tree which went on existing in spite of the fact that there was no logical necessity for it and in spite of the loathing which Roquentin felt for it.[1] But, as Kostelanetz remarks, in Sartre, as in Camus, "the surface is too realistic, the sense of human causality too conventional; and the characters, along with the reader, deduce absurdity from the course of credible events."[2] In other words, Sartre's characters, for all their unconventionality of behaviour, are real men in real situations, even when they try to make absolutely arbitrary decisions in order to assert their absolute independence and to be their own creators in a Godless and lawless world. Like André Gide's Lafcadio, who murdered a man against whom he had no grievance, simply in order to perform an entirely unconditioned and arbitrary act, an *acte gratuit*[3], their actions, however unconventional when judged by ordinary standards, are such as might conceivably take place in the actual world. But, to quote Kostelanetz again, "truly absurd literature does not discover meaninglessness; from its opening moments it accepts the condition and presents it as a theme.... It embodies absurdity in both the small events and the

[1] *La Nausée* (Eng. trans. *The Diary of Antoine Roquentin*).
[2] loc. cit.
[3] *Les Caves du Vatican* (Eng. trans. *The Vatican Cellars*), part V.

entire vision, in both the subject matter and the form"[1]. Thus, for example, by no stretch of the imagination could we conceive Mr Samuel Beckett's *Waiting for Godot* as actually taking place; as a scene from real life it is as impossible as a Wagnerian opera. Again, consider M. Eugène Ionesco's *Amédée or How to Get Rid of It*, in which a middle-aged couple have had their bedroom occupied for thirteen years by a corpse which is immune from physical decay but increases in size by an exponential law; this is clearly related to the world of common experience only in a highly symbolic way. To take a third example, when Mr John Barth wished in his novel *The Sot-Weed Factor* to express his complete distrust of human testimony and historical research, he did this by taking the story of John Smith and Pocahontas and rewriting it; however, he did not rewrite it in a more probable form that that of the traditional myth, but in one that was quite fantastically improbable and devoid of any evidential basis whatever. As Kostelanetz says:

> In mocking the conventions of the eighteenth-century novel by over-using them to such absurd lengths, in suggesting that the history we know is as unlikely as his rewriting of it, in doing both these things with such imaginative wit and breadth of reference, Barth ultimately says that not only are the single events of life preposterous – that is, absurd –

[1] loc. cit.

but also that life as a whole, which resists any order-
ing interpretation, is similarly, at base, absurd. Amid
all these facts Barth has only one truth, that there is
no truth.[1]

(In other words, for John Barth the Ministry of Truth
of George Orwell's *1984* is the world itself.)

To find a parallel to our present-day absurdists, we
might have to go back behind Sartre and Camus to
Franz Kafka. Kafka's unfinished novel *The Castle* is
about man's sense of being homeless in a meaningless
world; this is vividly and exasperatingly depicted in
the story of the repeatedly frustrated attempt of the
principal character, who is significantly denoted only
by the author's own initial "K", to gain admission
to the castle in which he believes, but is never quite
sure, that he has been appointed as land-surveyor. The
setting and the atmosphere of unreality and inconclu-
siveness are no less fantastic than those we find in
Ionesco or Arrabal, though the individual incidents are
slightly less phantasmagorean.

Now it would be a serious mistake to suppose that
these writers, in their assertion that the world is basically meaningless, are in general frivolous or cynical,
though they have no doubt attracted as many elements
of *pastiche* and *panache* as any other group in literature
or art. Many of them are men of a moral earnestness
that most conventional people will find it hard to credit

[1] art. cit., p. 708.

and still harder to account for. Both Gide and Sartre place a deliberate stress upon the importance of sincerity; indeed it is part of Sartre's thesis that it is only in utterly sincere, though arbitrary, human acts that any kind of moral significance can be brought into a world that is altogether contemptible and worthless. In the Introduction from which I have quoted, Esslin, like Lord Russell many years ago in his famous essay "A Free Man's Worship",[1] sees something fine and inspiring in the spectacle of man facing a hostile or indifferent universe in an attitude of heroic pessimism and defiance, with his head bloody but unbowed:

> The challenge behind this message [he tells us] is anything but one of despair. It is a challenge to accept the human condition as it is, in all its mystery and absurdity, and to bear it with dignity, nobly, responsibly; precisely *because* there are no easy solutions to the mysteries of existence, because ultimately man is alone in a meaningless world. The shedding of easy solutions, of comforting illusions may be painful, but it leaves behind it a feeling of freedom and relief. And that is why, in the last resort, the Theatre of the Absurd does not provoke tears of despair but the laughter of liberation.[2]

It would not be difficult to point to examples of the novel and the theatre of the absurd which do not seem in any normal sense of the words, to be noteworthy for

[1] Reprinted in *Mysticism and Logic.*   [2] op. cit., p. 23.

C

either dignity, nobility or responsibility, but rather to be expressions of filth for filth's sake, of sheer *nostalgie de la boue*; it would, however, be quite unfair to make this into a general rule. On the other hand, we ought not to forget that there is a great deal of modern literature which does not belong to the school of absurdity and which, without being either superficial or sentimental, breathes a more serene note. Not all serious writers to-day would feel that their message to mankind was most effectively communicated through the medium of a scene in which two of the four characters were permanently deposited in dust-bins. There are, I believe, truths about the world and about human nature that the absurdists have overlooked. Nevertheless, I believe that we have a lot to learn from their work, and as much from the fact that it exists as from what, if anything, it is trying to say. I do not think a sufficient explanation of the movement is to be found in the disappointments and frustrations of political and social history since the Second World War; the roots in any case lie farther back. Nor is it sufficient to dismiss the absurdists as a pack of neurotics and drug-addicts, for even if some of them are, the fact that they are may be significant. I would in fact suggest that the doctrine of the absurdity of existence is the natural climax of the process of secularisation which has increasingly characterised the thought and activity of the modern world. That is to say, if you try to find the ultimate meaning of the world simply within it you will fail, and then, if you refuse to look for it anywhere else, you will say that the world does not make sense. If you develop a neurosis as a result, this will be the effect of your conclusion rather than its cause.

I believe that the moral anarchy which has become more and more a feature of our community – the violence, the sensuality, the rapacity, the duplicity, with the ever-present background of frustration and neurosis – is to be explained by the fact that so many of our contemporaries, both young and old, seek without success to find a meaning for life in the only place where their secularised environment has taught them to look for it – namely in the world itself. This does not mean that we ought to encourage a revival of religion in order to get people to behave as we would wish; that would be to put the cart before the horse, as well as to degrade religion. For if people will not behave themselves because they love God, they are not likely to take up loving God as a help to behaving themselves; nor is there any reason why they should. What I do maintain is that the moral collapse of our community should not surprise any Christian believer; what would be surprising would be its absence. Indeed there *is*, I suggest, something surprising in the fact that people do not behave worse than they do; it indicates that, built into the unconscious springs of their conduct, there is a sense of the fundamental meaningfulness of life which on the conscious level they would be hard put to justify. Nevertheless, the restlessness and the homelessness remain in a setting of unparalleled material prosperity and secular satisfaction. Taken in itself, with all its resources and its unlimited offers of self-realisation, the world has proved to be a fraud and a lie; and its victims are subjects for compassion rather than condemnation. This, at least, the absurdists have seen, even if they have failed to see anything else.

The diagnosis which I have made of the situation may well seem to need justification, for it may be objected that science has found a great deal of sense in the world and has achieved a success in manipulating it such as no previous age in human history has known. This is indeed true, but it needs to be pointed out, without any disparagement of science, that the kind of meaning which science is concerned to discover is never an *ultimate* meaning. Science is interested in the way in which the world behaves and not with the world's ultimate nature; and, in spite of the sometimes unfortunate dabblings of scientists in philosophy and theology, this is as true of cosmology as of chemical engineering. Science is concerned a great deal with what men can do with the world, but not at all with the world's ultimate significance. It can discover a great deal about man's origin, his physical constitution and his genetic possibilities, but nothing about the basic reason – if there is one – for his existence. All its successes – and they are admirable and worthy of all praise – have in fact been due to this self-denying ordinance under which science has placed itself. It can ask, and can frequently answer, every question except the final one. It is therefore not surprising if, in a world which to an ever-increasing extent manifests the triumphs of science and has come more and more under its domination, its inability to give an answer to the ultimate question has led many to conclude that there is no answer to be given.

Nor has philosophy done very much to help the situation, except to help men to close their eyes to it. For a quarter of a century now, in the English-speaking countries and those under their cultural influence, the view that the primary, and indeed the sole, concern, of philosophy is to clarify our use of words has been almost unchallenged; "almost" I say, because the collection of essays made by Dr H. D. Lewis and published under the title *Clarity is not enough* has revealed that the linguistic citadel is beginning to crumble from within. To the outer world, however, the façade gleams with almost untarnished splendour, and with the necessary changes we might apply to our leading philosophers the words which N. P. Williams used of the official priesthood of the first-century Roman Empire, that "a Roman who was oppressed by the enigma of the universe, by the weight of unmerited misfortune, or by the sense of personal guilt, would no more have thought of applying to the *flamen Dialis* or to the *quindecemviri sacris faciundis* for ghostly aid and comfort than of confiding in the Prefect of the Praetorian Guards."[1] Nor has the exist-

[1] *Essays Catholic and Critical*, p. 385

entialist philosophy, which has flourished greatly on the Continent of Europe and has influenced much American theology, any light to throw upon the world or the human race as a whole. It invites each individual man to make his own existential choice, to affirm himself against a meaningless environment and so to bring about his own creation, but it has nothing to say about men as distinct from the individual man, and nothing to say about the world in which they are set; each man makes his own oasis in the desert. Sartre indeed tried to argue that his existentialism was effectually a form of humanism[1], but he is not generally thought to have succeeded[2]. The same judgment must, I think, be passed on those Christian existentialists such as Dr Kenneth Hamilton, who, following in the steps of Kierkegaard, see each man as confronted by God with the demand for a totally personal response, in which he and no one else is involved. The consequence is that nothing can be said about mankind in general; each man has to respond to God in his own personal encounter, but there is nothing in common between God's demand on one man and on another. The man himself achieves a meaning when he responds to God, but mankind and the world remain meaningless and irrelevant.

[1] *L'Existentialisme est un humanisme* (Eng. trans. *Existentialism and Humanism*).

[2] Cf. F. Temple Kingston, *French Existentialism: a Christian Critique*, chs. viii, ix.

Now the Boyle Lecturer, while he is to prove the Christian Religion "against notorious Infidels, namely Atheists, Theists, Pagans, Jews and Mahometans" – a sufficiently comprehensive assignment – is instructed "not to descend lower to any controversies that are among Christians themselves". I must therefore refrain from discussing whether there can be a genuinely Christian existentialism and must return to the point from which I digressed, namely that, whatever their weaknesses may be, the absurdists have given vivid expression to one truth of supreme importance, that the world does not make sense of itself. This point can be made as a purely philosophical point, about the existence of beings in general, as it was made by the early Wittgenstein, in a passage which his admirers have tended, with some embarrassment, to dismiss as an adolescent lapse into "mysticism":

The sense of the world [he wrote in his *Tractatus*] must lie outside the world. In the world everything is as it is, and everything happens as it does happen: *in* it no value exists – and if it did, it would have no value. . . .

All that happens and is the case is accidental. What makes it non-accidental cannot lie *within* the world, since if it did it would itself be accidental.

It must lie outside the world.[1]

[1] *Tractatus Logico-Philosophicus*, trans. Pears and McGuinness, § 6.41.

The senselessness of the world may on the other hand be expressed as a personal psychological reaction of disgust or loneliness, as in plays and novels of the school of absurdity, in Beckett or Ionesco. Or the two aspects, the philosophical and the personal, may be brought together in one account, as in the case of Sartre's hero Antoine Roquentin, for whom the chestnut-tree is both a logical monstrosity, in its sheer unaccountability, and also a violation of his own demand to be omnipotent, in its persistence in existing regardless of his will in the matter. What right has an object that is logically unnecessary to exist in Roquentin's world – if Roquentin wills that it shall not?

At this point you may, I think, well be wondering what all this has to do with the subject of these lectures. I want to suggest that there is a direct connection between the fact that writers such as those I have mentioned claim that the universe and human life are absurd and meaningless and the fact that they are atheists. But this is a point that it will take me a little time to develop.

Some well-meaning people in the past have argued for belief in God by maintaining that the world and human life, taken just as we find them in their bare character as objects of our experience, make perfectly good sense as they are. They have then argued from this starting-point that such a world must be the work of a being who is himself perfectly rational, intelligible and good, who is, in fact, what we mean by the word "God". This was the line taken by those seventeenth- and eighteenth-century thinkers whom Robert Boyle described, when he established this Lectureship, as "theists" but whom we usually describe by the rather similar word "deists"; I am afraid it was also taken by Robert Boyle himself. However, as Dr R. S. Westfall has shown in his book *Science and Religion in Seventeenth-century England*, the final result of this movement was to get rid of God altogether. For first of all, if the universe was really as perfect as the deists made it out to be, it would seem to be quite capable of accounting for itself; as Laplace is said to have replied to Napoleon, when the Emperor asked him why his work on mechanics made no mention of God, there was no need for that hypothesis. And secondly and more seriously, there is a great deal in the world that suggest it is by no means as perfect as the theists, who for the most part lived in comfortable and sheltered surroundings, assumed. The great Lisbon earthquake of November 1st 1755 shook the simple faith of the eighteenth century in the cosiness of human existence in a way that we, with our memories of greater upheavals, may find it difficult to understand. Nevertheless, well into the nineteenth-century Mrs Trimmer, in her little book for the instruction of the young, could reassure her infant charges that one of the reasons why a good God allowed earthquakes in Italy was in order that we might recognise how lucky we were not to have them here, and that in any case there was nothing like lava for producing a rich and fertile soil.[1] Now, the point that I want to make here is this: if you try to maintain either that the universe is self-explanatory or that it is morally perfect you can only do this by ludicrously distorting the facts, while, on the other hand, if you *could* do this satisfactorily, so far from having found grounds for believing in God, you would have rendered him unnecessary. In the words of M. Jacques Maritain, "Leibnitz pretended to justify God by showing that the work which proceeded from the hands of that perfect Workman was itself perfect, whereas in reality it is the radical imperfection of every creature which best attests the glory of the Uncreated."[2]

What I am arguing, therefore, is that the modern absurdists are fully right in maintaining that the world does not makes sense of itself. Where I think they are wrong is in assuming that nothing can make sense of it. I think also that, in order to get their point across, they frequently fall into exaggerations and one-sidedness. After all, life is not lived entirely in dust-bins, even symbolical ones; and chestnut-trees can inspire feelings other than those of disgust and resentment, as the crowds that flocked every year to Bushy Park would testify. Nevertheless the fact remains that, if the world

[1] *Easy Introduction to the Knowledge of Nature and Reading the Holy Scriptures, adapted to the Capacities of Children*, 15th ed., pp. 110f.

[2] *Religion and Culture*, p. 40.

is to be given a meaning, that meaning must come from some source outside the world itself. This is the lesson which we can learn from the absurdists, and there is, I believe, a direct connection between their determination to maintain that the absurdity of the world is ultimate and their atheism.

Herr Josef Pieper has perceived this very clearly in the case of Sartre. The latter, as we have seen, denies that things (and this includes persons as well) have any determinate and permanent "natures" and that there are any modes of behaviour that are simply proper to man as man. Things as they are are fundamentally inexplicable, and therefore they offer an insult to our reason; a human being is just what he makes himself from instant to instant, and so his conduct should be governed by no laws. But there appears to be a very interesting difference between Sartre, at least in some of his moods, and the majority of our absurdists. They seem to deny the existence of God on the grounds that the world is clearly so radically absurd that even God could not make sense of it. Sartre, on the other hand, (and this is also true of Camus) seems to deny that the world's absurdity could ever be surmounted because he is determined to be an atheist and has a lurking feeling that if there were a God he *might* make sense of it. Thus he is quoted as asserting: "Existentialism is nothing more than an attempt to draw all the conclusions from a consistently atheistic position" and: "There is no such thing as human nature, because there exists no God to think it creatively."[1] Which of the two – ultimate absurdity and atheism – is cause and which is effect may thus be disputed. And I am certainly not asserting that the atheism of Sartre is simply due to satanic pride and egotism; whether that is so or not is a matter between Sartre and his Maker (assuming that Maker exists), and on that I am not called upon to judge. But that the two things are connected is, I think, plain, and I would summarise my argument to the point that we have now reached as follows:

The existentialists and absurdists (who are very largely the same people) are, I believe, quite right in asserting that the existence of the world has no reason that can be found *within* the world itself. They are also, I believe, right in asserting that human life has no ultimate meaning that can be found *within* human life itself. They are, I believe, wrong in asserting that no reason can be found for the existence of the world *outside* the world itself; and they are, I believe, wrong in asserting that human life has no ultimate meaning that can be found *outside* human life itself. That these two problems – the problem of the existence of the world and the problem of the meaning of human life – are connected is, I suggest, vividly manifested in Sartre's story of Roquentin's encounter with the chestnut-tree; in fact I would maintain that the problem of the meaning of human life *is* simply the way in which the problem of

[1] *L'Existentialisme est un humanisme*, pp. 94, 22, cit. Pieper, *The Silence of St Thomas*, pp. 57, 58.

the world's existence bears upon the individual man or woman in his subjective singularity. And the final choice is between ultimate irrationality and meaninglessness on the one hand and a transcendent ground of rationality and meaningfulness on the other. Such a transcendent ground is identified by Christians and by theists in general (I am now using the word "theist" in the modern sense and not in Robert Boyle's) with the personal creator and sustainer of the world to whom they give the name "God". We have not, however, here reached the point of making that identification. I have drawn the material of my argument mainly from modern novels and plays, since we are often told today that it is the novelists and the dramatists who have the genuinely deep insights into reality rather than the philosophers and theologians.[1] What I have tried to show is that the world in which we live and of which we are part does not make sense of itself. So we are presented with this choice. We may, if we so decide, make the best of a world which is in the last resort a senseless and hostile desert, in which we must either bury our heads in the sands or make, each for himself, our little private oases. Or we may look for the world's meaning in some order of reality outside and beyond it, which can do for the world what the world cannot do for itself.

This second way is the way which I am inviting you to follow.

[1] Cf. H. E. Root in *Soundings*, p. 18.

CHAPTER THREE

The Vision of Glory

IF THE WORLD'S EXISTENCE IS TO RECEIVE AN ultimate explanation and if human life is to be given an ultimate meaning, that explanation cannot be found within the world itself and that meaning cannot be found within human life itself; they must be found outside. This is the point which we reached in the last lecture. I might have developed my argument in a strictly philosophical way, and if so I should have been following a great and impressive tradition of Christian thought, going back behind St Thomas Aquinas in the thirteenth century to St Anselm in the eleventh, and behind St Anselm in the eleventh to St Augustine in the fifth. Or I might have gone back to the Old Testament, to the book Ecclesiastes, in which the writer, having sought satisfaction in sensual delights, in good works and finally in the pursuit of knowledge, concludes that all the good things of this life lead only to disillusionment – "Everything is emptiness and clutching at the wind" – and that, if life has any meaning, that meaning can only be given it by God. I chose, however, to illustrate my theme from the literature and drama of the present day, rather than from formally philosophical works, for it seems to me that it is in plays and novels that the basic questions which we have to face are put before us most insistently. Miss Germaine Greer, discussing Mr John Grillo's play *Hello-Goodbye Sebastian* writes: "This play . . . deals, I think, with the light of every man in a world which is neither of his making nor of his choosing"[1], and here she has put her finger on the point where the wound smarts. Every man finds himself in a world which he has not made and which he has not chosen.

Now many of our contemporaries, including, perhaps, most of our contemporary philosophers, playwrights and novelists, would say that here we have the ultimate absurdity, the fact of which there is no explanation, the question to which there is no answer; but this seems to me to be a very odd position in which to rest. For it means that we can hope to receive answers to every conceivable question about the world and human life which our innate curiosity can suggest to us except the final and ultimate question, the question on which everything else depends, namely, why is there a world at all and what does human life ultimately mean? And I think it is very much to the point to remark that, throughout its history until quite recent times, the great mass of mankind has never been content with an ultimate irrationality and meaninglessness. Human religions have indeed been of the most astounding variety, but, until the rise of modern secularism, it seems to have been natural to man to recognise that, behind and beyond the world that our senses perceive,

[1] *Cambridge Review*, 29th May 1965.

there is another realm of being which, unlike the world of our senses, requires no explanation, and which, in some way or another, confers explanation upon the world of our senses and gives meaning to human life. Indeed, throughout history this has seemed to human beings to be too obvious to need argument. No doubt it is possible to give various reasons for the almost complete absence of this awareness at the present day. Marxists and the people who arrogate to themselves the title of scientific humanists will tell you that man has at long last managed to break the shackles of superstition that have bound him for millennia and has now come of age; he has been given the key of the front door and can live his own life in his own way. Another interpretation – and it is this that I myself would favour – is that our urbanised technocratic civilisation has atrophied a faculty which is really natural to man, so that we have now become incapable, without a great deal of deconditioning, of seeing something that is really just under our noses and which was as plain as a pikestaff to our ancestors. I cannot argue this in any detail at the moment, but I would just make two points. The first is that, as a matter of scientific anthropology, belief in a world beyond that of our sense-experience is one of the things that in fact distinguishes man from the beasts; it is indeed perhaps the most striking of these things. Even the highest of the apes are without it; even the most primitive of mankind possessed it: I recommend to you on this point Mr Leslie Paul's book *Nature into History*.

Entry into the spiritual [he writes], is an illumination to man of the terms and potentialities of his own mortal life, and . . . once launched into it he is separated from nature and can in no way return to that state of pristine innocence about the world and about itself which belongs to the animal in nature. Put that way, the entry into the spiritual dimension is a revelation of that which is beyond nature and is pulling man out of it. . . . The truth seems to be that the human entry into the spiritual is a growth into awareness of the ultimate realities of the universe. . . . The more one ponders the mystery of man, the less probable it seems that one misshapen Hominoid blundered into the realm of the specifically human, and the more probable it is that man was *called* into it, or even *commanded* into it.[1]

Modern atheism and secularism, therefore, do not mark a further step forward in man's progress to fully adult stature; they are a retrogression behind even the condition of infancy to the level of existence of the beasts. My second point – and it is here that our absurdist writers, whether intentionally or unintentionally, teach us their lesson – is that the emancipation of man from belief in the supernatural does not bring happiness but despair; and, for all the talk about the liberation that comes from looking the facts fearlessly in the face, imprisonment, rather than liberation, would

[1] op. cit., pp. 191, 193.

D

seem to be the appropriate term to describe it. In Samuel Beckett's *Endgame*, poor blind Hamm being wheeled by Clov round the walls of the little room that is his world, and his parents Nagg and Nell confined to their dust-bins, are not conspicuous examples of liberation. If modern man has acquired the key of the front door, he is very unsuccessful in turning the lock. The salvation that we are being offered is, in fact, nothing more than that gospel of pessimism which has been summed up in the statement that, in a world where everything is so bad, it must be good to know the worst.

Now we might at this point compare the beliefs about the supernatural realm that have been held by the great world-religions, and I hope in the course of these lectures to make this comparison. But I think it will be more interesting if, at this point, I make a leap forward and ask you to turn your attention to the Christian answer to this question of the ultimate reality that gives meaning to the world and to human life. And the answer of orthodox Christianity is this: the ultimate reality is God the Holy Trinity.

In saying this, have I already lost your sympathy? Have I seemed to offer a self-contradictory God as the explanation of an absurd world? May I ask you to be patient for a few moments?

I imagine that a great many people, if asked "What is the Trinity?" would begin their answer with the words "It is the doctrine that . . .". And I suspect the question would conjure up in their minds the picture of a group of senile and bearded clergymen – though beardedness today is perhaps as characteristic of the young as of the senile – sitting round a table and thinking up ways of making the Christian religion difficult for the laity. "Ah, I've got an idea", they imagine the most long-bearded and senile of the party twittering, as he sucks his toothless gums, "Let's tell them that God is both three and one; that'll give them something to swallow."

Now the first point I want to make is that the Trinity is not a doctrine at all. There is a doctrine *about* the Trinity, as there are doctrines about many other facts of existence, but, if Christianity is true, the Trinity is not a doctrine; the Trinity is God. And the fact that God *is* Trinity – that in some deep mysterious sense there are three divine Persons eternally united in one life of complete perfection and beatitude – is not a piece of mystification thrust by dictatorial theologians down the throats of an unwilling but helpless laity; and therefore to be accepted, if at all, only with reluctance and discontent. It is the secret of God's most intimate life, into which, in his infinite love and generosity, he has admitted us; and it is therefore to be accepted with amazed and exultant thankfulness. The way in which the Church, as it reflected on the life and teaching of Jesus of Nazareth and its experience of his liberating activity, was led to formulate its belief in the best words at its disposal is an interesting subject for Church historians; it must not detain us now. What we are concerned to see is what the Trinity means as an answer to the problem of the ultimate explanation of the world's existence and of the ultimate meaning of human life.

It means that the world and human beings depend for their existence from moment to moment upon the unfailing creative activity of a personal Being of unimaginable splendour, bliss and love. I have said "a personal Being" and not "a Person", only for this reason: that, if Christianity is true, God is not one Person but three Persons, united in one life of perfect mutual giving and receiving, a giving and receiving that is so complete that there is nothing to distinguish one from another except the ways in which each gives and receives from the others; a life of sharing so perfect that the most intimate of human unions bears only the remotest comparison to it. The belief that the world's ultimate explanation is to be found in a Being of infinite splendour, bliss and love is open to immediate and obvious objections, and we must not gloss them over. In particular we must face the problem of evil in all its sickening horror; how could a God who was absolutely powerful and loving allow babies to be born without limbs, or men to destroy one another's personalities by brainwashing? But problems such as this arise after you have come to believe in God, and not before. At the moment I want to ask you to consider how unutterably glorious is a view of existence that sees the ultimate reality with which each one of us is concerned as a Being such as I have described, rather than as the cribbed, cabined and confined existence of poor Hamm in his one little room and of his parents in their dust-bins.

It has become customary in some circles to ridicule the use of images in religion, but it is difficult to see how we can avoid them. The very people who pour scorn on the picture of heaven as a place where a celestial orchestra performs unending symphonies for the glory of God and the delectation of the redeemed will in many cases tell you that the most intense delight which they know is that of listening to music; and how can we more fittingly express our enjoyment of God than by comparing it, however inadequately, with the greatest of our earthly pleasures? Again, it is significant that the church has adopted the luxuriant nuptial imagery of the Song of Solomon as an analogy of the love of God for man and of man for God; for our enjoyment of God in heaven will be more, not less, ecstatic than the most passionate sexual experience on earth. And, if we want to acquire some remote understanding of the wonder and glory of the Christian God, we may well find the poets more helpful than the theologians.

Here, then, is Dante, in the final canto of the Divine Comedy, striving to put into words his vision of the triune Godhead, as it smote him in all its dazzling splendour, gathering into its one embrace all conceivable perfections, and in its threefold mystery eternally flooding itself with love. (I quote from Miss Barbara Reynolds's translation.)

The piercing brightness of the living ray
  Which I endured, my vision had undone,
I think, if I had turned my eyes away.

But I recall this further led me on,
  Wherefore my gaze more boldness yet assumed
Till to the Infinite Good it last had won.

O grace abounding, whereby I presumed
  So deep the eternal light to search and sound
That my whole vision was therein consumed!

In that abyss I saw how love held bound
  Into one volume all the leaves whose flight
Is scattered through the universe around;

How substance, accident, and mode unite
  Fused, so to speak, together, in such wise
That this I tell of is one simple light. . . .

And so my mind, bedazzled and amazed,
  Stood fixed in wonder, motionless, intent,
And still my wonder kindled as I gazed.

That light doth so transform a man's whole bent
  That never to another sight or thought
Would he surrender, with his own consent;

For everything the will has ever sought
    Is gathered there, and there is every quest
Made perfect, which apart from it falls short. . . .

Not that the living light I looked on wore
    More semblances than one, which cannot be,
For it is always what it was before;

But as my sight by seeing learned to see,
    The transformation which in me took place
Transformed the single changeless form for me.

That light supreme, within its fathomless
    Clear substance, showed to me three spheres,
        which bare
Three hues distinct, and occupied one space;

The first mirrored the next, as though it were
    Rainbow from rainbow, and the third seemed flame
Breathed equally from each of the first pair. . . .

Eternal light, that in Thyself alone
    Dwelling, alone dost know Thyself, and smile
On Thy self-love, so knowing and so known. . . .

The love that moves the sun and the other stars.[1]

[1] Dante, *The Divine Comedy* (Penguin Classics edition), III,
pp. 345ff.

This does not mean, however, that the vision of the divine glory can be a perpetual and unbroken experience in this life. Even the great Christian mystics profess to have seen the unutterable splendour only for the briefest moments, and much of their life has been spent in the aridity – the chastening and purifying aridity – of the Dark Night of the Soul. It is by revelation, rather than by direct experience, that the Christian is assured that the hidden reality which provides the world's existence with its explanation and gives human life its meaning, is the ineffable and inexhaustible splendour of the Holy Trinity. But once the glory has been glimpsed the memory of it remains, and the writings of the mystics are vibrant with the heartbreak and the yearning for its return and its full possession. "Whither hast vanishèd", exclaims St John of the Cross, the greatest of the Spanish mystics and one of the greatest of the lyric poets of Spain,

Whither hast vanishèd,
  Belovèd, and hast left me full of woe,
And like the hart hast sped,
  Wounding, ere thou didst go,
  Thy love, who follow'd, crying, high and low? . . .

O that my griefs would end!
  Come, grant me thy fruition full and free!
And henceforth do thou send
  No messenger to me,
  For none but thou my comforter can be. . . .

My love is as the hills,
   The lonely valleys clad with forest-trees,
The rushing, sounding rills,
   Strange isles in distant seas,
   Lover-like whisperings, murmurs of the breeze.

My love is hush-of-night,
   Is dawn's first breathings in the heav'n above,
Still music veiled from sight,
   Calm that can echoes move,
   The feast that brings new strength – the feast of love.[1]

"In this age of anxiety and violence", writes Mr Arthur C. McGill, "glory is out of fashion, even in the churches."[2] But only if we recognise that the God of Christianity is a God of utter glory and splendour can we understand the intensity and the concentration with which, down the ages, men and women have sought for union with him. The anxiety and violence of this present age are not a sign of vigour and vitality, but rather of frustration and enfeeblement. Our desires are not too intense but too weak, too dissipated and undirected. You may perhaps remember Mr Don Marquis's poem "The Lesson of the Moth", in which Archy, the cynical and disillusioned cockroach, describes how he had tried unsuccessfully to convince a moth of the foolishness of the latter's determination to "break in to an electric light bulb and fry himself on the wires".

[1] *The Spiritual Canticle,* trans. E. Allison Peers.
[2] *The Celebration of Flesh,* p. 184.

it is better to be a part of beauty
argued the moth,

for one instant and then cease to
exist than to exist forever
and never be a part of beauty . . .
and

records Archy,

before i could argue him
out of his philosophy
he went and immolated himself
on a patent cigar lighter
i do not agree with him
myself i would rather have
half the happiness and twice
the longevity
but

– and here the cynic gives himself away –

at the same time i wish
there was something i wanted
as badly as he wanted to fry himself.[1]

archy.

But, suppose you can be a part of beauty, not merely
for one instant but forever; suppose you can have *all*
the happiness and *all* the longevity, then could any
effort be too great in order to attain this end? Suppose
you can enjoy the very life of God——. And suppose
this flame is one that does not destroy but transforms

[1] *archy and mehitabel*, xxv.

and transfigures, that gives not death but life——.
Listen to St John of the Cross again:

O living flame of love
　That, burning, dost assail
　　My inmost soul with tenderness untold,
Since thou dost freely move,
　Deign to consume the veil
　　Which sunders this sweet converse that we
　　　hold. . . .

And O, ye lamps of fire,
　In whose resplendent light
　　The deepest caverns where the senses meet,
Erst steeped in darkness dire,
　Blaze with new glories bright
　　And to the loved one give both light and heat!

This is, I am well aware, not a popular approach to
the Christian religion at the present day. Is it not widely
asserted that the modern Christian must find God *within*
the secular order and not "outside" or "above" it? I
have just been quoting from St John of the Cross, but
was not he a cloistered Carmelite, a man who in order
to cultivate his own soul had fled from the world to the
safety of the monastery? And in a world where, in
spite of our vastly expanded technology, millions of men,
women and children are undernourished, uneducated
and diseased, is not all this talk about the glory and the
splendour of God sheer escapism and romanticism? I

shall have something to say later about the life of the contemplative religious, and I hope to show that it is very far from being an escape from the hard facts of life, a flight from reality. But on the general issue I should like to quote some words from one of the most perceptive and influential of modern Christian writers on the Continent, the Swiss priest Dr Hans Urs von Balthasar. In his book *Science, Religion and Christianity*, he writes as follows:

> Only those Christians who are most deeply aware of [the] utter transcendence of God will be able to interpret to modern atheists their own experience of existence with some hope of success. . . . Modern man has had the frightful misfortune that God in nature has died for him. Where religion once flowered like a blooming meadow, there is nothing left now but dry clay. Perhaps it is better so; perhaps that religion was like the Pontine Marshes that had to be drained. Nevertheless, the effect remains crushing. The Christian is not allowed to avoid this experience. He shares it as a human being. . . . The resurrection from this tomb is not brought about by reforms of the Church, but by a change in the mentality of the individual, returning to the origins of his religion. . . .
>
> This is not to say that the natural experience of contemporary humanity must from the start be interpreted in view of the Passion. This will be one of the

concluding aspects, but by no means the only one. Before any Christological interpretation of the time, God's majesty must stand out as the unchangeable background on which the diverse mysteries of Christ are outlined. . . . The meaning of our time is that God should be exalted higher above contemporary man who himself occupies a higher position than before, and that man thus exalted should in his turn fall down more humbly before this infinitely exalted Lord. Christians must be more intensely on fire with the love of God; they will have to be so if possible more absolutely, more silently, with less dramatic gestures and forms of devotion, which might still be tolerated in the Baroque period, but became impossible in the nineteenth century. . . .

Everything depends on this poverty towards God and in God, poverty of God in us. . . . Then it rests with God whether this "poverty in spirit" is to be experienced as felt or as unfelt "bliss", whether man feels himself incredibly enriched by God's infinity or robbed of all finite things without being aware of having gained God.[1]

This is splendidly said, with its insistence that, in a secularised world, Christians must not play down the transcendence of God but must, on the contrary, accept it into their own thinking and living and proclaim it by their lives. And yet I wonder whether, in stressing this

[1] op. cit., pp. 101ff.

necessary truth, von Balthasar has not left something out of the picture. For God is not only the transcendent being before whom all his creatures must fall in silent homage; he is also self-existent joy and bliss, and his joy and bliss, no less than his transcendence are manifested in the world that he has made. My argument up to this point has been that, in the last resort, neither the world nor human life make sense of themselves, and I have illustrated this from the drama and literature of our day. Nevertheless, I do not want to bring God in simply at the fifty-ninth minute of the eleventh hour, to prop up from outside a world that is tottering into absurdity. And I want now to stress that there is much in the world that suggests that it is the creation of a God of supreme loveliness and beauty. As I pointed out in the last lecture, life is not lived entirely in dust-bins, even symbolical ones, and chestnut-trees not only inspire feelings of disgust and resentment in French existentialists but manifest exquisite beauty to ordinary people.

> I think that I shall never see
> A poem lovely as a tree,

wrote Joyce Kilmer; and went on to add:

> Poems are made by fools like me,
> But only God can make a tree.

Even on the level of brute experience, the world is not merely squalid, widespread as squalor undoubtedly is. It is a world in which exquisite beauty is to be found, beauty in the things of nature, beauty in the artefacts of man, beauty in human behaviour and human relationships. But this beauty is uniformly imperfect, impermanent and, on its own level, inexplicable. It is only understandable in terms of Creation and the Fall. St Augustine has the reputation of having been a somewhat austere Christian, but to him the most heart-rending feature of the world was the fact that so much beauty was fragile and fugitive; and it could only be understood at all as reflecting the visage of a Creator who was supremely beautiful and changelessly eternal. "All this fabric most fair, of things that are truly good, will pass away when its course has been completed; they have their morning – and their evening."[1] And so he turned to God with the cry: "Late, how late have I loved thee, Beauty ever old and ever new."[2] And St John of the Cross, as we have seen, is exuberant in his application of imagery derived from the natural world to the God for whom he yearns:

My love is as the hills,
    The lonely valleys clad with forest-trees . . .

Or, again:

Rare gifts he scatterèd
    As through these woods and groves he pass'd apace
Turning, as on he sped,
    And clothing every place
    With loveliest reflection of his face. . . .

[1] *Confessions*, XIII, xxxv.   [2] ibid., X, xxxviii.

The creatures, all around,
　Speak of thy graces as I pass them by.
Each deals a deeper wound
　And something in their cry
　Leaves me so raptur'd that I fain would die.[1]

Has ever such haunting expression been given to the
sense that the beauty of the natural world is both an
effect and a reflection of the uncreated beauty of its
Maker?

Nevertheless, the fact must be emphasised that our
awareness of God in this life is, at any rate for the most
part (for moments of mystical intuition may be com-
moner than has sometimes been supposed), very partial
and fragmentary, and its full enjoyment lies beyond the
grave. "Here we see in a mirror, dimly; but then face
to face."[2] And we shall not discern him if we restrict our
gaze to the surface of things and make no attempt to
become sensitive to the deeper realities. "The things of
the Spirit . . . are spiritually discerned."[3] If we look only
for the dust-bins, we shall see only them; for they are
certainly there. And if we see only them, the absurdity
of the world will seem to be ultimate, for the world
does not explain itself. But if we look for the world's
explanation beyond itself and find it in a God who is
infinite and self-existent love, bliss and splendour, then
we can look back on the world and see it bathed in his

[1] *Spiritual Canticle*, trans. Peers.　　[2] I Cor. xiii. 12.
[3] I Cor. ii. 14.

beauty and reflecting it from its myriads of facets. But even as we look at him we shall be dazzled by him, and his splendour itself may appear to us as darkness. With the Apostle we may say "I could not see for the glory of that light",[1] and shall seek someone to lead us by the hand. And the more we come to know him, the more we shall recognise how much there is of him we do not know. With the Psalmist we may exclaim: "He made darkness his secret place, his pavilion round about him: darkness of waters, thick clouds of the skies."[2] God is indeed mystery, but without him we have not mystery but absurdity. "The true alternative", it has been well said, "is not mystery or clarity, but mystery or absurdity."[3] In Abbot Vonier's words: "It is an indispensable condition of all true and lasting admiration that its object should be greater than our knowledge of it; and the growth of knowledge, far from touching the limits of the marvellous, should convince us more and more of their inaccessibility."[4]

God is infinite love, bliss and splendour; and, because he is infinite love, he wills that his bliss and splendour shall not be enjoyed by him in isolation but that there shall be other persons who shall share in it and enjoy it, if they will accept it as coming from him. The Christian God is not like the First Mover of the Greek philosopher Aristotle, totally absorbed in self-admira-

---

[1] Acts xxii. 11.   [2] Psalm xviii. 11.
[3] C. B. Daly, in *Prospect for Metaphysics*, ed. I. T. Ramsey, p. 204.
[4] A. Vonier, *Collected Works*, I, p. 107, cit. Daly, p. 205.
E

tion and not even conscious that the world exists, as the world does its own poor, pathetic best, by its own feeble efforts, to imitate the perfection – the cold and arid perfection – which it beholds in him. The Christian God is a God who, while he is absolutely self-sufficient and perfect in his own life of love as Trinity, nevertheless pours out upon creatures the superabundance of that love. "Behold, I have graven thee upon the palms of my hands."[1] "I have loved thee with an everlasting love."[2]

This is the love that moves the sun and the other stars.

[1] Isaiah xl. 16.   [2] Jeremiah xxxi. 3.

CHAPTER FOUR

Not without Witness

G. K. CHESTERTON WAS ONCE INSPIRED TO WRITE
an amusing little poem by a newspaper paragraph
which expressed the fear that a missionary in the
Pacific, who had suddenly disappeared, might have
been cooked and eaten, as there had been, to use the
paper's own words, "a considerable revival of religious
customs among the Polynesians".

> It was Isaiah Bunter
>   Who sailed to the world's end,
> And spread religion in a way
>   That he did not intend.
>
> He gave, if not the gospel-feast,
>   At least a ritual meal;
> And in a highly painful sense
>   He was devoured with zeal.

This may suffice to remind us that religion can take
very varied forms, some of which are not wholly com-
mendable. Rising above the primitive cultural level of
the Polynesians, we may remember that the very highly
developed Aztec civilisation of Mexico, which was still
flourishing when America was first discovered by
Europeans in the fifteenth century, was overshadowed

by a grisly cultus centred in human sacrifice. The existence, throughout history down to the present day, of witchcraft and devil-worship, too, may correct any tendency to assume that all religions are really the same and that all are equally good or, alternatively, equally bad. On the other hand, it is preposterous to dismiss the great non-Christian religions of the world as mere error and confusion, on the grounds that grace and truth came by Jesus Christ and that all that is not of faith is sin. St Paul, at the very moment when he was appealing to his pagan hearers to turn from vanities to the living God, told them that in no nation had God left himself without witness. And in recent years, when the religions of Asia, Judaism, Islam, Hinduism, Buddhism, Confucianism and the rest, have been studied more and more thoroughly, it has become possible to fill out this general statement – that in no nation had God left himself without witness – with detailed knowledge that makes it possible to approach them sympathetically and constructively.

I shall, therefore, ask you now to consider the question: what should be the attitude of the Christian as he approaches these other great faiths? First of all, we must not think that because God has been fully and uniquely revealed in Jesus Christ, no knowledge of God is to be found outside Christianity or that God is not free to reveal himself as and where he sees fit. If we can find in some Hindu or Mohammedan circles beliefs which we recognise as being true, we should welcome this joyfully. If, indeed, we discover that many devout Hindus or Mohammedans have been more faithful and consistent in following the light that has been given them than we have been in following the light that has been given us, we should accept this gladly and gratefully; we must neither belittle it on the one hand nor be embarrassed and resentful on the other. What is above all necessary when we approach the non-Christian religions is that we should honestly try to discover exactly what their teaching is, and then see how that teaching is related to the teaching of Christianity. We need have no fear that if we do this we shall be endangering the uniqueness of Christianity; on the contrary, we shall be able to see more accurately the respects in which Christianity is unique. St Augustine did just this with the Neo-Platonic philosophy of his day. That philosophy believed in a triad of entities which it called the "One", the "Mind" and the "World-soul", and it seemed to St Augustine that these were virtually the same as the Father, the Son and the Holy Spirit of the Christian Trinity. "Therein", he wrote – that is, in the neo-Platonic writings – "I read, not indeed in the very words, but to the very same purpose, enforced by many and divers reasons, that In the beginning was the Word, and the Word was with God, and the Word was God. . . ." And so he goes through the verses in which St John describes the life of the Word with the Father in eternity, and the creation of the world by the Word in time. And then he is brought to a stop: "But that he came unto his own, and his own received him not . . . this I read not there." And again: "I read there that God the Word was born not of flesh or of blood, nor of the will of man, nor of the will of the flesh, but of God. But that the Word was made flesh and dwelt among us I read not there."[1] So when we find in the Hindu Vedanta that Brahman – the supreme self – is "Being, consciousness, joy", we may well recognise an adumbration of the revelation that God is Trinity, for these three words correspond fairly closely to the characteristics that Christian theologians have seen as belonging to the Father, Son and Holy Spirit. But that the "Consciousness" became incarnate, in the sense in which Christianity believes that the Son became incarnate – that we read not there. Judaism and Islam believe in an absolutely transcendent God, but the idea that such a God could become man seems to them to be altogether ridiculous and blasphemous. Many forms of Hinduism, on the other hand, believe in incarnation and reincarnation, but the God in which they believe is really identical with man or with the world to begin with. It is the special and shocking announcement of Christianity that in Jesus of Nazareth a God who is absolutely self-sufficient, and who has created the universe by an act of pure love, has, for us men and our salvation, taken upon himself our created nature and has himself become man.

And just because of this, just because Christianity

[1] *Confessions*, VII, xiii, xiv.

believes that God is the universal creator and the universal saviour, it must also claim that every particle of truth that is found in the religions of mankind comes from this same God and therefore is not to be despised but to be welcomed. Furthermore, we must not be surprised, though we may well be ashamed, if some of the great religious figures of Hinduism or Islam have shown a deeper insight into the facets of the truth that have been given them than we Christians have as yet acquired into the fulness of truth that has been revealed to us. For to penetrate to the heart of the truth of God, it is not enough to have been given it; you must love it, cling to it and live by it. Again, if Christ is the saviour and perfecter of the whole human race, the full manifestation of the riches of Christ will require for its expression all the outlooks, aptitudes and capacities of mankind, and not only those of that one culture to which we belong. And if this is so – if the manifestation of Christ in human thought and life requires the contribution of all the races of the world – the question inevitably poses itself, as to what God has been doing in the religions that have not explicitly accepted Christ. If Christianity is to welcome into itself the cultures of Hinduism and Islam, must we not recognise that God has already been preparing them for their reception, and that he has been moulding them for the special contributions that they will be able to make to the Christianity of the future? I should like to recommend to you very warmly a little book by a Christian priest of mixed Hindu and Christian parentage, Dr Raymond Panikkar. Why his book *The Unknown Christ of Hinduism* is so valuable is because it insists that, although it is very important to investigate the similarities and the differences between Christian and Hindu *beliefs*, the real question that we have to face is, "What has Christ been *doing* in Hinduism?" Thus he goes so far as to write: "The good and *bona fide* Hindu is saved by Christ and not by Hinduism, but it is through the sacraments of Hinduism, through the message of morality and good life, through the *Mysterion* that comes down to him through Hinduism, that *Christ* saves the Hindu normally. This amounts to saying that Hinduism has also a place in the universal saving providence of God."[1] And we must make a similar judgment on the other great religions, Islam, Buddhism, Confucianism, Taoism and the rest, while we must remember that a special place belongs to Judaism; for Judaism has the unique status of being the womb within which Christianity itself was conceived, and from which it was born.

This universality of Christ's redemptive and perfecting work has been splendidly expressed in the Decree on the Church issued by the Second Vatican Council in November 1964:

In the first place stands the people that was given the covenants and the promises [that is, the Jews]; they were the human stock from which Christ took his

[1] op. cit., p. 54.

origin. . . . But the design of salvation also includes those who recognise the Creator, and among them especially the Moslems; it is their avowal that they hold the faith of Abraham, they join us in adoring the single, merciful God who will judge mankind at the last day. Then there are men who are seeking the God they do not know, in shadowy imaginings; God is not far from men of this kind, for he gives to all men life and breath and all we have, and it is the Saviour's will that all men should be saved. There are men who are in ignorance of Christ's gospel and of his Church through no fault of their own, and who search for God in sincerity of heart. . . . They do so under the influence of divine grace, they can attain everlasting salvation. Nor does divine Providence deny the necessary helps to salvation to men who, through no fault of their own, have not yet reached an express acknowledgment of God, yet strive with the help of divine grace to attain an upright life.[1]

Nevertheless, the Decree utters two sharp and salutary warnings, first that outside the Church men may only too easily fail to respond to the grace of God and fall either into vice or into despair, and secondly that within the Church men may only too easily fail to co-operate with the grace that they have received and fall under judgment more severe.[2]

[1] *Dogmatic Constitution on the Church*, para. 16.
[2] ibid., paras. 16, 14.

In speaking thus I am only asking that we should today approach the great world-religions and their cultures in the same spirit in which the Church in its early days approached the religions and cultures which then confronted it. This spirit was not uncritical; the Church was well aware of the dangers that it faced in baptising the thought and outlook of Greece and Rome. Indeed, the struggle of the Church with heresies such as Gnosticism and Arianism shows this. And no doubt the thought and outlook of Hinduism and Islam, when in God's good time they come into the Church, will produce, side by side with their harvest of good grain, a new, and perhaps even more persistent, crop of heresies. But the point remains, that the unchanging Faith needs to be expressed in ever-changing forms, and if the task of communication is to be successful those forms must be taken from the thought and outlook of the contemporary world. Twice in its history the Church has performed the task with striking success: when it baptised the thought of Platonism in the first five centuries, and when it baptised the thought of Aristotelianism in the thirteenth. The transition from the first of these to the second did not prove too difficult, in spite of temporary suspicions and disputes, for the two had much in common; and the enduring monument to its achievement is the writings of St Thomas Aquinas. In embracing the new insights the Church lost something, but not a great deal, of the old. Far less successful was her assimilation of the third great cultural change, which

came in the seventeenth century with the sudden explosion of the scientific method. The change was too
abrupt and the Church herself was weakened and per-
plexed with schism, and we today live in the aftermath
of that failure, with several centuries of backlog to
recover. Furthermore – and this is a point that some of
our present-day reinterpreters do not sufficiently understand – the radically secular outlook that our Western
civilisation has now acquired is far more difficult to
baptise than was that of the ancient world, for the latter
was basically religious, even if often pervertedly so, and
ours is not.

It is far more difficult for us in England today than it
was for Christians in the past to interpret the Faith to
the contemporary world and to assimilate contemporary culture to the Faith. This is no ground for
despair, but it is a ground for healthy realism.

I have, however, digressed from our main topic in
this lecture, namely the attitude of Christianity to the
other great world-religions. What will be precisely involved in the interpretation of Christianity to Asia and
Africa we cannot possibly foresee in detail, any more
than St Paul could foresee the *Apology* of St Irenaeus or
the *Summa Theologiae* of St Thomas Aquinas. And the
main burden of the task must be borne, not by European
or American Christians trying to understand Hinduism
or Islam, but by Hindu or Islamic Christians who have
fully grasped the essence of Christianity; this is where a
book like Dr Panikkar's is so useful. This does not mean,

of course, that the great achievements of European Christianity have no lessons to offer; they have many, and not all of them are dreadful warnings. Such monumental achievements of the Christian intellect as St Augustine's *City of God* or St Thomas's *Summa* are not to be discarded as merely useless or troublesome. But neither are they simply to be translated word for word into Asian languages and applied like a poultice. Both our problems and our resources are greater than we sometimes recognise.

Now if we want to see the real essence of any religion we must look at the witness which is borne by those hundred-per-cent practitioners of it whom we know by the name mystics. In what I now have to say I shall rely mainly on the researches of Professor R. C. Zaehner, whose writings combine a passionate attachment to orthodox Christianity with a deep and sympathetic insight into the great religions of the Asian world; in particular I recommend to Christians of any denomination his small book *The Catholic Church and World Religions*. Professor Zaehner points out that there are three types of mystical experience in which men have claimed to have penetrated to the reality behind the world of our everyday experience.[1]

The first is nature-mysticism. In this the world as a whole – and this, of course, includes our own selves – is seen as consisting of bubbles on the surface of a universal divine substance, so that in order to achieve

[1] op. cit., pp. 17ff, 132ff.

perfect satisfaction and beatitude we must sink beneath the level of sense-experience and lose our personal identity by merging ourselves into this undifferentiated impersonal unity. Most types of Hinduism are of this kind, and so, it would appear in Professor Zaehner's view, is the Chinese Taoism. One of the best-known modern examples of this is provided by Richard Jefferies whose book *The Story of my Heart* has become a minor English classic; the French poet Jean-Arthur Rimbaud provides another. May I quote from Jefferies a short passage in which he describes his experience:

> Gradually entering into the intense life of the summer days – a life which burned around as if every grass blade and leaf were a torch – I came to feel the long-drawn life of the earth back into the dimmest past, while the sun of the moment was warm on me. . . . From all the ages my soul desired to take that soul-life which had flowed through them as the sunbeams had continually poured on earth. As the hot sands take up the heat, so would I take up that soul-energy. Dreamy in appearance, I was breathing full of existence; I was aware of the grass blades, the flowers, the leaves on hawthorn and tree. I seemed to live more largely through them, as if each were a pore through which I drank. . . . I was plunged deep in existence, and with all that existence I prayed.[1]

Two points here are of deep importance. First, for all

[1] op. cit., ch. I.

his talk of prayer, Jefferies did not believe that there was anyone to pray to; prayer was for him simply a psychological technique for uniting himself with the impersonal divinity of the universe. Secondly – and this is very significant indeed – together with this desire to unite himself with the very stuff of existence, there was a terrifying discovery that the stuff of existence, the impersonal divinity, was not interested in man and was, indeed, hostile to him:

> All nature, the universe as far as we see, is anti- or ultra-human, outside, and has no concern with man. . . . Centuries of thought have failed to reconcile and fit the mind to the universe, which is designless, and purposeless, and without ideas. . . . There being nothing human in nature or the universe, and all things being ultra-human and without design, shape, or purpose, I conclude that no deity has anything to do with nature. . . .

So, in the end, with a brave but half-hopeless yearning, this man who sought, and seemed to have found, complete satisfaction in nature can only hope for "something better than a god".

> There is something superior, higher, more good. For this I search, labour, think, and pray. If after all there be nothing, and my soul has to go out like a flame, yet even then I have thought this while it lives. With the whole force of my existence, with the whole force of my thought, mind, and soul, I pray to find this

Higher Soul, this greater than deity, this better than God.[1]

Nowhere, to my knowledge, has the ultimate hollowness, the final disillusionment, of nature-mysticism been so heartrendingly expressed as in these words of the great nature-mystic. Is there not here an implicit appeal to a God above and beyond the world's own substance, a God who, unlike the great god Pan, is not a god with cloven hoofs? I may remind you in passing of E. F. Benson's story "The Man who Went too Far". In this a nature-mystic who had achieved a life of remarkable loveliness and compassion, was found, at the very moment when he had expected the nature-god to reveal himself to him in all his beauty and glory, lying bruised and dead, with his skin marked with pointed prints, "as if caused by hoofs of some monstrous goat that had leaped and stamped upon him"[2].

The second type of mysticism is very different. In it the human soul is convinced that neither in the world nor above it is beatitude to be found, and it practises a technique of self-isolation; it descends into the depths of itself and tries to find fulfilment there, cut off from all other beings and from everything except the bare experience of its own being, its own self-identity. This, too, is to be found in Hinduism. Both the Roman Catholic Zaehner and the Jew Martin Buber have diagnosed it in the same way from the standpoint of belief in a personal

[1] ibid., ch. iv.
[2] See the volume of stories *The Room in the Tower*.

God. What the mystic is experiencing is in fact his own self, which is made, as the Book Genesis tells us, "in the image of God"[1]; but, because he does not recognise it as such, he takes it to be the ultimate reality and so tries to find ultimate satisfaction in it. What God may do for such a soul it is not for us to say; but in itself such a condition can only be judged by a theist as self-condemnation to ultimate frustration and misery, to the solitude of hell. In Zaehner's words: "The experience is entirely confined to the individual self and makes impossible all communion with other men or with God; it is the deadest of all possible dead ends."[2] And he quotes Martin Buber to the same effect.

It was, one can hardly doubt, the recognition that neither of these ways can lead to ultimate happiness that took Gautama Buddha even farther along the negative road. Later Buddhism has proved unequal to the demands of the Master and has sometimes even made him into a God, but it appears that his own teaching was one of radical despair. "Call no man happy until he is dead", said the ancient Greek sage Solon[3]. But what if men survive death? And what if they are born again into this world each time they die? If life is fundamentally misery, death is no guarantee of escape, for there may be life after death; there can be only two ways of escape, extinction and sheer insensitiveness. Students of Buddhism have disputed whether

[1] Genesis 1, 27.   [2] *The Convergent Spirit*, p. 101.
[3] Herodotus, *Histories*, i. 32.

the technique which Gautama expounded is intended to lead the disciple to "cease upon the midnight with no pain" or to reach a condition in which he is entirely indifferent to everything, including his own survival or non-survival; but it is plain that what is sought is a kind of spiritual suicide. Gautama himself seems to have been one of the most exquisitely self-forgetful and compassionate men who ever lived – a perfect example of the "man for others" – and his decision to postpone his own achievement of *Nirvana* for the sake of teaching his method to others is beyond all praise.

Again, it is not for us to say what God can make out of such sincerity and selflessness. But of the basic Buddhist doctrine we can only say that it mistakes the inability of human life to make sense of itself for the inability of God to make sense of it, since, as it holds, there is no God. Strict Buddhism may thus be closer than would appear on the surface to our modern literary and dramatic absurdists; and the evident attraction which Zen Buddhism has had for the American Beat Generation may not be entirely a pose or a fad. It should also be noted that the atheism of Buddhism is a passive rather than an active atheism; and many students hold that, although it does not include God, it does not on the other hand exclude him. For this reason both M. René Guénon and Dom Aelred Graham have suggested that a theistic, and indeed a Christian Buddhism, is in principle possible.[1]

[1] Aelred Graham, *Zen Catholicism*, pp. 14f.

F

The third type of mysticism is, as Zaehner says, "something quite new: it is the personal encounter of the transcendent self with the living God and the realisation of his infinite love . . . the soul's love affair with God to which there can be no end."[1] And this, from the Christian point of view, is the authentic type. That a God who is in himself absolutely self-existent and transcendent should, even if he is also in himself the fullness of personal being, want to take his creatures up into his own life might seem to be more than we have any right to hope; and neither Judaism, Mohammedanism nor Protestant Christianity have found it an easy notion to accept. It has seemed to involve either the degradation of God to the level of his creation or else the destruction of the creature and its transformation into another god. It is therefore all the more striking that in Islam itself, the religion in which more than in any other, the absolute and unqualified supremacy of God over his creatures is declared – the word "Islam", we may remember means simply "submission" – there should have arisen a school of mystics – the Sufis – who have claimed that a human being can, without in any way ceasing to be a creature and as such utterly dependent upon God, be taken up into a life of the most intimate personal union with God and can be transformed in the flame of God's love. The most striking instance of this is that of Al-Hallaj, who was crucified at Baghdad in A.D. 921. He was accused of having claimed

[1] op. cit., p. 133.

in moments of ecstasy to have "become God", but scholars seem to be agreed that in fact he was a genuine theistic mystic who can be compared without detriment with the great mystics of Christendom. More striking, still, is the fact that, in Hinduism as well, there have been teachers and mystics who have believed in a personal God and in the possibility of man achieving beatitude in union with him. The astounding manifestation of Krishna in the *Bhagavad-Gita*, and the teaching of Ramanuja in the eleventh century, show how, even in Hindu thought, belief in a personal God, in whom alone man's ultimate satisfaction is to be found, can make itself felt when the setting is favourable – or, should we rather say, when God sees fit to reveal himself?

It is, however, in the great Christian mystics of both the Eastern and the Western Church that we find the clearest and most rapturous expression of personal mystical union, a union which, may I remind you again, is often achieved at the cost of great suffering and spiritual darkness and which demands a supreme degree of detachment.

> O living flame of love
>> That, burning, dost assail
>>> My inmost soul with tenderness untold . . .

And here may I touch upon several points of first importance in connection with this personal and most authentic type of mysticism.

First, the God with whom it is concerned is neither an impersonal ground of the world nor the substance of the mystic's own soul, but is the *personal* God of eternal love and bliss who is the Blessed Trinity; therefore there is no hard-and-fast infallible technique for achieving the mystical union. Relations between persons depend upon free-will on both sides; all that the potential mystic can do is to prepare himself or herself to be ready for the mystical experience if it should please God to give it. And, since that preparation consists in loving and obeying God, it is not essentially different from any attempt to live whole-heartedly as a Christian.

Secondly, and following on from this, however much difference there may be between the *experience* of the Christian mystic and that of the ordinary devoted Christian, there is no real difference in their basic *condition*; as Fr Garrigou-Lagrange writes, "the mystical life is the Christian life which has become somehow conscious of itself."[1] As Professor Zaehner says, "Every time we go to Holy Communion, so long as we are in a state of grace, we share in God's own godhead – we are 'deified'. We are not conscious of it: the mystic is. Therein lies the difference."[2] For – and here I quote Mr E. I. Watkin: "The way from sanctifying grace to beatific glory is one continuous road of increasing supernatural union between the soul and God."[3]

---

[1] *Perfection chrétienne et Contemplation*, I, p. 149.
[2] *The Catholic Church and World Religions*, p. 18.
[3] *Philosophy of Mysticism*, p. 129.

Hence, thirdly, for the Christian, mystical experience, in the strict sense of the word, is never necessary, either for salvation or for sanctity, as it tends to be in the non-Christian religions. If I can find beatitude only by merging myself in the impersonal ground of being that lies beneath the world that my senses experience, or if I can find beatitude only by isolating myself from everyone and everything other than myself and then turning my gaze inward to the depths of my own soul, then clearly I must concentrate my efforts on its achievement in a thoroughly self-interested way. I must apply myself to its techniques with the same unsparing single-mindedness as an athlete training for the long-jump or a cosmonaut training for a space-flight. But if beatitude consists in union with a personal God who is self-existent Love and Bliss, then I shall achieve union with him by making a loving response to his love in obedience and faithfulness, and this may or may not involve my adopting an unusual or solitary mode of life. I may be called to the cloister, like St John of the Cross; I may be called to a life of poverty and service in the slums of Paris, like Mother Maria Skobtsova[1]; I may be called to the perfectly ordinary life of the office, the factory, the school or the home. For, since God himself is my beatitude, I shall achieve beatitude not by seeking beatitude but by seeking God; and seeking God means, above all else, doing his will. And, in this modern world, seeking God in ordinary life may be as exacting,

[1] Cf. *One, of Great Price*, by Sergei Hackel.

and indeed may be far more exacting, a task than seeking him in the cloister or the desert.

Nevertheless, the Church will never be able to do without those whom God calls to serve him in what is technically called "the religious life", for it is they who keep before the eyes of Christians the fact that it is in God alone that the meaning of human life is to be found, and their example may preserve us from the ever-present temptation to put God's gifts in the place of God himself and to try to find our ultimate satisfaction in them instead of him. Some of the great ascetics of Christian history may puzzle and even repel us, partly because they are on a different wave-length from ours and partly because their very intensity of love may sometimes lead them into excesses. But we must remember that they are people who are consumed with love for God, and people who are in love often do things that appear ridiculous to outsiders and are sometimes ridiculous in themselves. When you read a book like *The God-possessed*, by M. Jacques Lacarrière, with its stories of men and women who went off to live in caves and tombs, on pillars and up trees, in their determination to be with God, pause from wondering whether their actions were guided by considerations of social utility, etiquette or hygiene – frequently they were not – and reflect on the intensity of their desire. Then you may ask yourself whether there is anything that you want as much as those men and women wanted God. (Remember Archy the cynical cockroach and his friend the moth, whom we considered in the last lecture.)

Further we must remember that even the stylite on his pillar or the dendrite up his tree is not performing his austerities simply for his own salvation; he is one with us in the human race and in the Body of Christ, and what he is doing he is doing not only for himself but for us. And among all the problems with which the religious communities are faced in the modern world, one thing seems clear – that God still calls men and women to the life of contemplative prayer. This leads me to my last point.

Surprisingly – though perhaps it is not really surprising – it seems to be true that the kind of prayer that is possible and fruitful for people who are living active lives in this present-day world is very much more like that of the enclosed religious orders than it is like that which for more than three centuries since the Reformation was taken as the obvious method both for active religious and for Christians in secular occupations. I can only give one illustration of this. When you are travelling on the Underground, as an alternative to gazing at the pipes on the walls of the tube, or trying to decipher your neighbour's newspaper, or even, as a last resource, reading the advertisements, you may not find it very difficult to practise a simple form of contemplative prayer. You will find it much more difficult to engage in pious meditation upon the childhood of St Aloysius Gonzaga.

And now may I bring you back to the point from which we started, namely, God's universal offer of himself to man.

CHAPTER FIVE

Paradise Regained

THE MOST IMMEDIATE CONCERN OF A NORMAL MAN or woman is with other human beings: with wife or husband, children, kinsfolk, neighbours, associates and clients at work, friends and acquaintances at play. Indeed, even when we were unconscious infants, we were dependent upon other people for our sheer physical survival; and probably the first visual objects which we learnt to recognise were our mother's breast and face. Individuals here and there may find themselves drawn, either by temperament or by vocation, to a solitary existence, but this is something abnormal. Even in the Egyptian desert in the early days of monasticism, hermits found themselves being drawn together into some form of cenobitic life; and it is significant that the noun which seems to go most naturally with the adjective "monastic" is in fact "community". Two of the most tragic conditions for any human being are, on the one hand, loneliness and, on the other, social maladjustment; that is to say, either the absence or the derangement of the communal relationship. Mr Harvey E. Cox, in his book *The Secular City*, has rightly pointed out that, in an urban community a man must distinguish between his private and his public relationships[1], since he

[1] op. cit., p. 41.

simply cannot be on intimate terms with everybody; but this means that urban community is not the same as rural community, not that it is not community at all. Most urbanites, Mr Cox remarks, "live a life in which relationships are founded on free selection and common interest, usually devoid of spatial proximity. . . . This does not mean the apartment dweller cannot love his next-door neighbour. He can and often does so, certainly no less frequently than the small-town resident. But he does so by being a dependable fellow-tenant, by bearing his share of the common responsibility they both have in that segment of their lives shaped by residence. This does not require their becoming cronies."[1] This is, I think, very true, and I would add that even the hermit in the desert, if his vocation is a genuine one properly accepted, is not simply cutting himself off from society, even for the salvation of his own soul; however little others may understand it, and even if he does not perfectly understand it himself, he is living the life that he is living for the sake of Christ's Body the Church.

Man, then, is a social being, and lives in a social context. Nevertheless it is a sheer mistake to suppose that his relationships are purely social ones and that he can fulfil himself by attending exclusively to the latter. By the very fact that he has a body, he is part of the world of nature as well as of the world of persons; as somebody has remarked, it is only by pushing lumps of matter into a hole at one end of him that he can keep alive at

[1] ibid., pp. 44f.

all. It is, I think, surprising how little attention some of our secularists, with the great stress that they place on existential personal relationships, seem to give to this equally obvious fact, especially since they are only too ready to appeal to the discoveries and assumptions of science against the doctrines of religion. For if there is anything on which scientists seem to be more or less agreed, it is that the human species is organically related to the evolutionary process of the planet on which it lives and, behind that, to the physical universe as a whole. No philosophy of human life can be adequate if it concentrates simply on the relationship in which the individual stands to other human individuals and ignores that in which he stands to the entire universe.

It is, I think, the recognition of this fact, after decades of neglect in religious circles, that mainly accounts for the extraordinary vogue at the present day of the Jesuit anthropologist and mystic, Pierre Teilhard de Chardin. As a scientist, his standing is, to say the least, controversial; against the exuberant commendations of Sir Julian Huxley[1] we can set the almost virulent denunciations of Dr P. B. Medawar[2]. As a theologian, his amateurishness was a constant source of anxiety to his religious superiors. The dithyrambics with which he acclaimed the explosion of the atomic bomb in the Arizona Desert in 1945[3] certainly lend colour to the

[1] Introduction to *The Phenomenon of Man*.
[2] Review of *The Phenomenon of Man* in *Mind*, LXX (1961), pp. 99ff. [3] *The Future of Man*, pp. 140ff.

suspicion that he underestimated the potentiality of man for evil as well as good, and in his writings as time went on he kept his Christianity more and more in the shadows, so that if we had not the remarkable confession of faith which was written three days before his death[1] we might almost wonder what had become of it. Nevertheless, with all these limitations, one thing stands out quite inescapably: that for Teilhard the whole process of the evolution of the universe was dominated by the two facts, that in it man was to appear and that in manhood the Creator was himself to become incarnate. Teilhard saw unique significance in the fact that man alone among earthly species had now reached the point of populating the whole of this planet: the "planetisation of man", as he called it[2], was an event of cosmic importance. "Zoologically speaking", he wrote, "mankind offers us the unique spectacle of a 'species' capable of achieving something in which all previous species had failed. It has succeeded, not only in becoming cosmopolitan, but in stretching a single organised membrane over the earth without breaking it."[3] Indeed, this "membrane", although it is not material but is constituted by man's intelligence, is spoken of almost as if it was a kind of plastic envelope restricting man to the surface of the earth. "I adopt the supposition", Teilhard wrote, "that our noosphere [this is the name that he gives to the "membrane"] is destined to close in upon

[1] ibid., p. 309.   [2] Cf., e.g., *The Future of Man*, ch. x.
[3] *The Phenomenon of Man*, pp. 241f.

itself in isolation, and that it is in a psychical rather than a spatial direction that it will find an outlet, without need to leave or overflow the earth."[1] Elsewhere he envisages the bare possibility that "we are destined by contact with other thinking planets, across the abysses of space and time, some day to become integrated within an organised complex composed of a number of Noospheres", but he describes this as seeming "infinitely improbable".[2] We may wonder what he would have thought about the developments which have taken place in astronautics since his death, or indeed what he thinks about them now. What is plain is that he thought of the next stage in man's career as converging towards a condition of mental unification which he denoted as "Point Omega". Just what he thought this would involve has puzzled his closest students, but it is clear that he held that there would be a union of consciousnesses without any loss of individuality. "The concentration of a conscious universe would be unthinkable if it did not reassemble in itself *all consciousnesses* as well as all *the conscious*; each particular consciousness remaining conscious of itself at the end of the operation, and even (this must absolutely be understood) each particular consciousness becoming still more itself and thus more clearly distinct from others the closer it gets to them in Omega."[3] Furthermore Teilhard insists that Point Omega is not just the last term in the series of man's

[1] ibid., p. 287.   [2] *The Future of Man*, p. 179.
[3] *The Phenomenon of Man*, pp. 261ff.

successive states of development; it is distinct from it and transcends it. Thus the final destiny of the human race is not a Hindu loss of individuality by immersion in deity, nor a Buddhist nirvana, but – though this is left to be inferred rather than explicitly stated – it is what the Christian tradition would describe as the vision of God in the Communion of Saints.

It is also clear that Teilhard sees Point Omega as already set up by the Incarnation of God in Jesus Christ. Its full manifestation as the climax of the world's history ("cosmogenesis", as Teilhard calls it) and of man's history ("noogenesis") will be seen only at the Last Day, but it already exists in Christ himself and this is what gives it its dynamic force. "If the world is convergent", Teilhard writes, "and if Christ occupies its centre, then the Christogenesis [the "building up of Christ"] of St Paul and St John is nothing else and nothing less than the extension, both awaited and unhoped for, of that noogenesis in which cosmogenesis – as regards our experience – culminates". And he sums this up in the magnificent sentence: "Christ invests himself organically with the very majesty of his creation." [1]

This notion of Christ as gathering up the whole process and history of God's creation was, we may recall, splendidly developed by the great Bishop of Lyons, St Irenaeus, who in all probability met a martyr's death about the year 200; he saw it implied in St Paul's assertion that it pleased God, in the fullness of time, "to sum

[1] *The Phenomenon of Man*, p. 297.

up all things in Christ, the things in the heavens and the things upon the earth".[1] And in the Eastern Orthodox Church the sense that the whole of the material order is in principle transfigured and transformed through the taking of a material body by God the Son is one of the most striking features of the Liturgy and of theology; the Feast of the Transfiguration of Christ is seen as the feast of the transfiguration of the whole of the physical world. We have found in Teilhard the word "Christo-genesis" as applied to the world's history; in the same context the Russian theologian Fr Paul Evdokimov has used the almost identical word "Christification" to describe the effect of the Incarnation on the whole human race:

> The formation of Christ in man [he writes], his Christification, is neither an impossible imitation nor the application to man of the merits of the Incarnation, but is the injection into man of the Incarnation itself, and it is brought about and perpetuated by the Eucharistic Mystery.[2]

But – and here I quote another Russian Orthodox writer, Dr Nicholas Arseniew:

> It is not man alone who is affected by the redemption and the joy of victory; with the joy over our resurrection is linked also joy over the redemption of the whole world, over the ending of the dominion of corruption, over the redemption of all creation and the

[1] Ephesians i. 10.   [2] *L'Orthodoxie*, p. 113.

dawn of the kingdom of life. And the eye of the
Spirit gazes fervently out towards the glory to come –
that "splendid freedom of the children of God" of
which all creation shall partake. [Is not this Teilhard's
"Point Omega"?] The resurrection is thus an event
of cosmic significance, and the world, equally with
man, is there permeated by the radiance of the
celestial glory, although as yet in hidden form, and
has attained to a new and high worth; for it has
already taken unto itself the germ of immortality.[1]

Or again, in the words of Vladimir Lossky:

The world was created from nothing by the sole will
of God – this is its origin. It was created in order to
participate in the fullness of the divine life – this is its
vocation. It is called to make this union a reality in
liberty, in the free harmony of the created will with
the will of God – this is the mystery of the Church
inherent in creation. Throughout all the vicissitudes
which followed upon the fall of humanity and the
destruction of the first Church – the Church of paradise – the creation preserved the idea of its vocation
and with it the idea of the Church, which was at
length to be fully realised after Golgotha and after
Pentecost, as the Church properly so-called, the
indestructible Church of Christ. From that time on,
the created and contingent universe has borne within

[1] *Mysticism and the Eastern Church*, p. 35, cit. A. M. Ramsey,
The Glory of God and the Transfiguration of Christ, p. 138.

itself a new body, possessing an uncreated and limit-
less plenitude which the world cannot contain. . . .
The entire universe is called to enter within the
Church, to become the Church of Christ, that it may
be transformed after the consummation of the ages,
into the eternal Kingdom of God. Created from
nothing, the world finds its fulfilment in the Church,
where the creation acquires an unshakable foundation in the accomplishment of its vocation. [1]

It is perhaps well at this point to emphasise that there
is nothing in all this that contradicts the hope in a
glorious destiny for the human race which we find in
the writings of scientific humanists such as Sir Julian
Huxley and Dr Waddington. With the appearance, in
the course of evolution, of the self-conscious rational
being man, evolution itself can set out upon a new
and vastly accelerated course. It is no longer subject
to the blind and wasteful operation of natural selection;
it can be planned by man. What Waddington calls
"socio-genetic" evolution is possible. The Christian
Faith does not deny this hope, but fills it with substance
and gives some grounds for supposing that it can be
realised. For the thorny problem of the scientific humanist is that, while science is on the verge of putting into
our hands quite terrifying powers of influencing the
nature and planning the future of the human species, it
provides no principles for deciding what future we

[1] *The Mystical Theology of the Eastern Church*, pp. 112f.

should aim at and no reasons for supposing that in any case we shall achieve it or even that the human species will survive. In contrast, Christianity holds that God's purpose in creating a world at all was that, in it and as part of it, there should be rational and intelligent beings capable of knowing and of loving him and of achieving entire satisfaction and beatitude in sharing his own life; and it also holds that God himself assumed their human nature, so that in order to share his life they should not have to do violence to the nature that he had given them but should on the contrary develop its potentialities to the full. In order that we should not have to leap out of our own skin in order to attain our end, he has leapt into our skin himself. Thus the future evolution of the human race – if "evolution" is not now too weak a term to use – is evolution *within Christ* – "Christo-genesis", "Christification", or, in the words of the Epistle to the Ephesians, it is "the building up of the Body of Christ, till we all attain . . . unto a full-grown man, unto the measure of the stature of the fullness of Christ".[1] The use of the singular number is significant; we are not to be full-grown *men*, but a full-grown *man*. It is the total Christ who is being built up out of his members; it is Christ who is "coming of age".

It is, I think, useful to consider how we are to view the traditional doctrine of the Fall of Man in the light of modern scientific theory. We are certainly not called upon to abandon it; we are, on the contrary, helped to

[1] Ephesians iv, 13.

see rather further than we could before into its nature and consequences. Professor Zaehner, viewing the emergence of man as a "gradual passage from sub-consciousness through group consciousness to self-consciousness – from the sense of belonging to the All and through All to its source which is God to total self-consciousness and self-confidence", sees this as resulting "not only in the isolation of man from his fellow men but also from any sense of intimate communion with his environment. The human race", he writes,

> was split up into fragments: in Biblical terms the "image of God" was shattered. Man, henceforward, being but a shattered fragment of the "All-Man", cut off from all intimate relationship with the whole, cut off too from any sure knowledge of God as the author of his being, had no alternative but to go it alone. At the same time, it may be assumed, he had memories of a life in which he was not conscious of his own individuality and in which his solidarity with the whole had guaranteed his own immortality in the context of the whole. His religious quest would there-fore now be divided: first he would try to restore his lost sense of solidarity through social means, since he no longer *felt* the oneness of all things, and secondly he would delve deep down within himself in a effort to discover immortality within his own being. Inter-mittently too a deep nostalgia for a vanished age of innocence would make itself felt and men would, on

rare occasions, catch a fleeting glimpse of a vanished golden age.

"To sum up, then", Zaehner concludes, "we may take the doctrine of the Fall as related in the Book of Genesis to mean the full emergence of the human race into consciousness."[1]

This is an extremely penetrating passage, for it provides a convincing and fruitful explanation of the main types of human religion, as we saw them in the last lecture. I think, however, that it has one weakness, though it is a weakness that can easily be corrected; Zaehner appears to be asserting that, with the emergence of man as a self-conscious being, sin – the Fall – was not merely possible but inevitable; and in this he unexpectedly aligns himself with those Protestant theologians who have been accused of virtually identifying creation with the Fall.[2] Rather I would wish to suggest that with the emergence of man there arrives an unprecedented possibility for both good and evil – the Grand Alternative. At last there is on earth a being who can either respond to the God of whom he is now conscious in an ecstasy of self-abandonment and love – and if he does this he will find himself caught up by the divine Lover and taken into God's own Life – or he can choose to shut himself up in his own being in a spurious self-

[1] *The Convergent Spirit*, pp. 62f.

[2] Cf. Reinhold Niebuhr on the Barthians, *Moral Man and Immoral Society*, p. 171; H. R. Mackintosh on Kierkegaard, *Types of Modern Theology*, p. 237.

sufficiency and condemn himself to frustration and con-
striction. The point has been expressed extremely well
by Dr J. V. Langmead Casserley, as follows:

They [that is, Adam and Eve in the Genesis story] are
naked food gatherers and their way of life is precisely
that which we must attribute to the very first human
beings. Resembling the higher primates to a remarkable degree, they pick berries from bushes, fruit from
trees, and dig edible roots from the earth. Their fall
is their primitive failure to make the leap from
innocence to righteousness at the point at which such
a step was necessitated by the process of their evolution, In a way innocence and righteousness are re-
markably alike; in another sense there is a decided
difference between them. Innocence is enjoyed in-
stinctively without forethought or deliberate will;
righteousness, on the other hand, must be consciously
willed and intended. Apart from this important dis-
tinction the actual content of innocence and righteousness is identical. They differ not in the content
but in the mode of their being. To become truly
human, to rise to the fullness of the new human
stature, a transition from innocence to righteousness
is absolutely essential. It was the failure to make this
leap with success that we call the fall, a falling short
of the indicated and necessary objective.[1]

[1] *Apologetics and Evangelism*, pp. 32f.

I should like to develop this point in the following way. According to Christian belief, it is of the essence of all created beings to be un-self-sufficient and dependent – dependent upon God at every moment of their existence for the loving activity by which he preserves them in being. This is in sharp contrast to the view that was commonly held by those philosophers in the ancient world who followed in the footsteps of Aristotle, that every being was a self-determined nature, containing in itself its own potentialities and needing nothing outside itself for its own existence. Creatures, as Christian thought envisages them, are not closed but open; their very continuance depends upon the fact that God incessantly pours into them their being. Beneath the conscious level they manifest this dependent status simply by following their law of their being, by acting as the kind of things they are. This is true of lifeless matter obeying physical law, and of living beings following the laws of vegetable growth or of animal instincts. When, however, we come to man we are faced with a totally novel and critical possibility; for, since he is self-conscious and has a sense of right and wrong, he, first among the products of the evolutionary process, can either obey or disobey the law of his being as he chooses. He can either accept his dependence upon God and turn to God in gratitude and loving obedience, and by so doing he will be acting in accordance with his nature; or he can rebel against it and claim the right to a self-sufficiency which he does not in fact possess. The former alternative is virtue – in Casserley's terms, the "transition from innocence to righteousness" – and if man had made it he could have been, and would have been, welcomed by God into an enjoyment of God's own life which would have brought him un-dreamed-of fulfilment and joy; the second alternative is sin, and it has produced the sad condition in which we are. In the light of this, two classic facts of Christian teaching stand out clearly: first, that sin is basically *falsehood*, it is, as we say, "acting a lie"; secondly, it is *frustration*, for it is fighting against the law of our own being. Division between man and man, and division within our own selves, are the natural consequence of man's separation of himself from God.

It is this failure, this rebellion, at the beginning of human history that accounts for the condition which theology describes by the term "original sin", the con-dition of alienation from God into which we are all born as members of the human race in this state of threefold dividedness. The problem how original sin is transmitted from one generation to another has, I think, been treated by theologians as more of a problem than it really is. When they have thought of human beings as separate isolated individuals, as they sometimes have, they have almost inevitably thought of original sin as a kind of disease or genetic defect inherited from one's parents in their act of sexual union, almost as if the sin of Adam and Eve had caused a mutation or mutations of genes in the chromosomes of their germ-cells. And then all sorts of problems, both ridiculous and repulsive, arise. But if, on the other hand, we remember that human beings are not separate isolated individuals but members of a family whose Father is God, then we shall see that the condition of original sin, of dividedness, which we inherit is not due to something having gone wrong with the mechanism of procreation but to the fact that the human race, into which we are born as members, is itself in a state of division – division from God and in consequence division within itself. This is not really a new theory, though we are perhaps in a position to have a clearer view of its meaning. It was plainly implied by St Thomas Aquinas as long ago as the thirteenth century, though he did not work it out as fully as we might wish. His point was that original sin is, in each of us, not a defect in his *person* but in his *nature*. [1] Now his person is what each of us has for himself; it is the seat of his incommunicable self-identity, what makes me *I* and not *you*. But his nature – his human nature – is what he shares with the whole human race; and he cannot come into a fallen and divided race without inheriting its common features, both good and bad. Furthermore, it was human nature, not a human person, that God the Son united to himself when he became man. Thus, both the state of fallenness and the state of redemption appertain in the first place to the human race as such, and then to individual men and

---

[1] Cf. the Appendices by T. C. O'Brien, O.P., to vol. xxvi of the new translation of the *Summa Theologica* (Blackfriars, 1964).

women as members of it; and this does not mean that God is not interested in us as individuals, but that he is interested in us as the kind of individuals that we are, namely members of one another.

The ultimate transformation of both the human race and the whole physical universe in Christ is, of course, extremely difficult for us even remotely to imagine. It lies far outside the range of our normal experience. But so, too, do many of the conditions in which scientists assure us many objects in the universe are at the present day. When we have become ready to accept without demur the statement that the temperature at the centre of a star may be something like one thousand million degrees Centigrade and that the atoms of which it is composed have been stripped not only of their electrons but also of particles from their nuclei under pressures of the order of 100,000 million million pounds per square inch, it hardly seems reasonable to cavil at the ultimate transformation which Christianity postulates simply on the ground that it is difficult to imagine. We have in fact one pointer to its nature, in the transformation which Christ's own individual body underwent at his Resurrection and Ascension. In this, as the records in the Gospels depict it, we see a human physical organism which is able, at will, either to function in a commonplace and familiar way or to transcend the limitations of commonplace human existence as we know it. The risen Christ can eat fish and honey with his friends and offer them his hands and side to touch;

yet he can pass through closed doors and vanish instantaneously, and finally withdraws himself, in the dazzling display of the Ascension, from sight and touch altogether. Now, if we admit that the status of the Christian is that of incorporation into Christ's human nature, and if the ultimate destiny of the material universe is to be, in some mysterious but nevertheless quite real way, taken up into Christ, the strain on our imagination will perhaps be less severe, and there certainly need be no strain on our faith. We shall come back to this point later on.

There is one more point that I must make. What are we to say about the possibility, to which scientists seem more and more to incline, that in some parts of the universe other than this planet (though almost certainly not anywhere in our solar system) there may be intelligent beings perhaps vastly more powerful and competent than ourselves? Teilhard seems to have been so enthralled by the potentialities of the human race on this planet that he never gave this question serious consideration. It seems to me, however, to need facing, though I cannot see that, whatever the answer may be, there is anything about it that should cause anxiety to a Christian. I have discussed this in detail in my book *Christian Theology and Natural Science*; I will only briefly summarise the conclusions here, and in doing so I should like to point out how very wide is the range of possibilities between which orthodox Christian doctrine leaves us perfectly free to decide.

Even if such beings [that is, rational corporeal beings other than man] exist, man may, for all we know, be the only corporeal creature who has fallen and needs redemption; Dr C. S. Lewis has made play with this notion in his novel *Perelandra*. Again, if they have fallen, the conditions both of fall and of redemption may be radically different from those that apply in the case of man. . . . There may or may not be somewhere in the universe rational beings other than man. If there are, they may or may not have fallen. If they have fallen, their redemption may or may not require that the Son of God should become incarnate in their nature. God may or may not have some other way of restoring them to fellowship with himself; he may perhaps have an even more wonderful way, of which we cannot form the remotest conception. Whatever may be the truth about this. . . . I cannot see any conclusive theological objection to the view that the divine Word may have become incarnate in other rational species than our own.[1]

On the other hand, it may be the case that, by becoming incarnate in one rational species, the Son of God has *ipso facto* become the redeemer of all.[2] About this we can speculate, but can do little more.

I would sum up this lecture by emphasising that the attitude to the physical universe and to human history

[1] op. cit., pp. 43f.

[2] Cf. R. J. Pendergast, "Terrestrial and Cosmic Polygenism", in *The Downside Review*, LXXXII (1964), pp. 189ff.

which orthodox Christianity offers us is one of unparalleled scope and richness. It does not provide neat and final solutions to all the problems which science can pose for religion; why, in any case, should we expect all our questions to be answered in ten minutes? It does, on the other hand, welcome and incorporate into itself the picture of the world that science has painted and also invests it with an ultimate meaning that science is incapable of giving it. Fr Karl Rahner has remarked that "human truth is of such a kind that even in theology to settle one question, even correctly, raises three new questions that remain to be settled"[1]; this is one of the things that make it so interesting to be a theologian or even to be a human being, and it ought certainly not to cause us any special anxiety. And I would conclude by reminding you that, even this great vision of the physical universe, as conceived by science and interpreted by Christian theology, is not the whole of the truth as Christianity understands it. For it is a Christian belief that the physical universe is only part of God's creation; that behind and beyond it there is a realm of purely spiritual beings, in whose affairs we have in fact become implicated. But I must leave this for my next lecture.

[1] *The Dynamic Element in the Church*, p. 76.

CHAPTER SIX

Unseen Warfare

IN THE LAST LECTURE WE WERE CONSIDERING THE stupendous theme that God's ultimate purpose for the human race and for the whole material universe is that they should be taken up into Christ and transformed into a condition of unimaginable glory, and that it is for this that God himself took our human nature, in which spirit and matter are so mysteriously and intricately interwoven. This theme – the theme of the Cosmic Christ – is expressed in the Epistle to the Ephesians in the assertion that it is God's good pleasure, in his management of the historical process (for that is what is meant by the phrase that the Authorised Version of the Bible renders as "the dispensation of the fullness of the times"), to gather together all things in Christ[1]; it is depicted even more majestically in the Epistle to the Colossians, where we are told that God's dear son is

> the Image of the invisible God, the firstborn of the whole of creation [that is, the son and heir who inherits all his Father's possessions]; for in him all things were created, those that are in heaven and those that are on earth, visible and invisible, whether

[1] Ephesians i, 10.

thrones, or dominations or principalities or powers [that is to say, spiritual beings as well as material]; all things were created through him and for him, and he is before all things, and all things are held together in him.

Furthermore we are told in this same passage that by his death on the Cross he has restored to union with God not only the human race but the whole created order. "In him we have redemption through his blood" indeed, but it is not only the human race that has been reconciled to God by the blood of the cross, but "all things, . . . whether they are things in earth or things in heaven"[1]. "Things in heaven and things on earth", "visible and invisible" – by such phrases we are reminded of the fact on which I touched at the end of the last lecture, that it is part of traditional Christian belief that, behind and beyond the physical universe, there is a realm of purely spiritual beings, in whose affairs we have become implicated. I need hardly recall to you the tremendous and superb imagery in which the last book in the Bible, the Revelation of St John the Divine, depicts the warfare in the unseen world between the angels of light and the powers of darkness.

I know very well that to many people today the mere mention of angels and devils will be sufficient to get one written off as pre-Copernican, if not indeed antediluvian, but I would ask you to consider whether this negative

[1] Colossians i, 15–20

reaction is not itself due to a combination of prejudice and misunderstanding, prejudice against believing in anything that is not a direct object of our senses, and mis-understanding about what in fact the Church has believed concerning good and evil spirits. About this particular prejudice I hope I have said enough already, but the misunderstanding needs more attention. First, may I make it quite clear that the Church has never held that the devil is a being equal to, but opposed to God, a kind of black and negative deity, related to God as a positron is related to an electron or a left-handed to a right-handed screw. Such a view has, indeed, persistently re-curred throughout the Church's history, but it has always been denounced by the Church as one of the most pernicious of heresies; its technical name is Mani-chaeanism, and Sir Steven Runciman has written a fascinating book about it[1]. Devils are fallen angels, and angels are God's creatures; and the Devil with a capital D is only the leader of a self-frustrating and hatred-ridden rabble. The fundamentally futile and incoherent nature of the diabolic enterprise has, I think, nowhere been so vividly and startingly depicted as by the late C. S. Lewis in his famous *Screwtape Letters*; like the damned in Dante's *Inferno*, they have "lost the good of the intellect", they have no more the desire or the ability to distinguish truth from falsehood but only an insati-able craving to do as much destruction as possible and in particular to absorb other personalities into their

[1] *The Medieval Manichee*

own. "To us", writes Screwtape to his nephew the young demon Wormwood,

> a human is primarily food; our aim is the absorption of its will into ours, the increase of our own area of selfhood at its expense. But the obedience which the Enemy [that is, God] demands of men is quite a different thing. One must face the fact that all the talk about His love for men, and His service being perfect freedom, is not (as one would gladly believe) mere propaganda, but an appalling truth. He really *does* want to fill the universe with a lot of loathsome little replicas of Himself – creatures whose life, on its minature scale, will be qualitatively like His own, not because He has absorbed them but because their wills freely conform to his. We want cattle who can finally become food; He wants servants who can finally become sons. We want to suck in, He wants to give out. We are empty and would be filled; He is full and flows over. Our war aim is a world in which Our Father Below has drawn all other beings into himself; the Enemy wants a world full of beings united to Him but still distinct.[1]

And yet, as a subsequent letter shows, the perverted demonic mind cannot convince itself that even God can really love his creatures:

> The truth is I slipped by mere carelessness into saying that the Enemy really loves the humans. That, of

[1] *Screwtape Letters*, viii.

course, is an impossibility. . . . All His talk about love
must be a disguise for something else – He must have
some *real* motive for creating them and taking so
much trouble about them. The reason one comes to
talk as if He really had this impossible Love is our
utter failure to find out that real motive. What does
He stand to make out of them? That is the insoluble
question.[1]

I must resist the temptation to quote more fully from
C. S. Lewis's brilliant book, which I am sure is well
known to most of you. I would only ask you not to take
it as some of my secularist friends insist on taking it, as
simply a brilliant *tour de force*, if not just an amusing
jeu d'esprit; that is exactly how the powers of darkness
would like you to take it. It is in fact a shatteringly
accurate analysis of the essentially predatory and nihil-
istic character of the activity of Satan and his mob. And
I would like to draw your attention to another book,
also by a lay theologian, which is largely devoted to this
subject, but which is less well-known than *The Screwtape
Letters*, Mr Gerald Bonner's small but concentrated
work *The Warfare of Christ*, and especially to its last
chapter. Mr Bonner points out that to dismiss belief in
demons is to do much more violence both to the New
Testament and to the experience of the Church than
appears at first sight. He comments pointedly on the
fact that a recent writer, having proved to the hilt that

[1] ibid., xix.

Jesus believed in demons, makes no attempt to discuss whether we ought to believe in them too, but asserts roundly that Satan is a symbol of "the malign power of man's societary life", which dominates him and destroys his personality.[1] Mr Bonner also points out that the same writer "in the almost contemptuous words 'the Satan of Medieval legend' . . . dismisses, not merely the supernatural tall stories in which the Middle Ages undoubtedly delighted, but the whole bulk of Patristic and Christian ascetic theology". He finally refers to a matter which it is difficult to get academic theologians to take seriously but which is more and more troubling those in positions of pastoral responsibility, namely "the experiences of those who have had to deal with persons or places in some way subject to demonic influences, whether by infestation, obsession or possession", and he urges very sensibly that "anyone who wishes to discuss the demonology of the New Testament ought to be prepared to consider the experiences of contemporary Christians who are in no way particularly credulous and superstitious, but who have had experiences of supernatural phenomena closely resembling the cases of demonical possession recorded in the New Testament".[1]

Having cleared the ground in this way, Mr Bonner remarks that, although belief in the devil is not one of the major articles of Christian belief, to ignore it may involve us in very disconcerting spiritual perplexities. "Given free will," he writes, "it is clear that an indi-

[1] Trevor Ling, in *The Significance of Satan*.

vidual can sin, even without any diabolical interven-
tion; but it is equally clear that, if devils exist, they may
be responsible for a sudden, unseen and unheralded
temptation. . . . Because we are fighting a war against
an adversary and not merely disciplining ourselves, we
must not necessarily expect any diminution in the power
of our later temptations. The last battles of a campaign
may well be as bitter as the first."[2] And he goes on to
argue that we just cannot afford to drop the third
member of the traditional division of sins as deriving
from the World, the Flesh and the Devil. After a
masterly discussion of the first two categories, he remarks
that the temptations that are essentially diabolic are
spiritual, not material, as the Desert Fathers were well
aware. "The demons make use of earthly inducements,
the beguiling visions of lovely women, the treasure
which St Antony found in his path; but when a monk
has passed beyond these temptations, a more terrible
adversary lies ahead: the temptation to Pride, the head
and fount of all sins, the sin by which Satan himself fell
from heaven."[3] But he adds that, in this century,
diabolically induced sin has taken two other very terrible forms. The first of these is the lust for power: "The
twentieth century has seen a new type of power-addict
emerge; the fanatic to whom the mere externals of
power mean little or nothing, who glories in the substance, in the naked actuality. If we turn to Hitler as our
example, it is not because he is the only instance, but

[1] op. cit., pp. 96ff.   [2] ibid., pp. 100f.   [3] ibid., p. 109.

because he is a particularly perfect specimen. About him and his circle there was a mean asceticism, a lack of any of the enjoyment of the good things of life which the Nazi despots could have enjoyed. . . . In this way he differs from other great war-lords of history.

"But even more terrible", Bonner goes on, "perhaps, than the power-worshippers are that other class of twentieth-century fanatics: the men obsessed with a monstrous ideal which they are prepared to carry to its logical conclusion without any qualms, themselves remaining basically dull, timid and respectable. An arch-exemplar of this horrible fraternity is surely Heinrich Himmler. This strange, dreary little man, frugal in his habits, honest in his finances, who disapproved of blood sports because they were cruel . . . was the head of what were, perhaps, two of the most evil organisations which the world has seen; the Gestapo and the S.S.; was responsible for the running of ante-chambers of hell like Belsen, Auschwitz, Dachau, Ravensbrück, and many others."

Bonner adds, as any Christian should: "I am not making any judgment upon his final destiny – who knows what may have happened in the instant between his biting the poison capsule and its inevitable effect? I do not doubt that, lacking grace, any of us might have behaved so differently from him; but it seems to me clear, beyond all doubt, that in him we have a man who was under an influence far deeper and more terrible than any temptation which the World or the Flesh could offer, and which I personally feel constrained to regard as something more personal and active than the 'spirit of unredeemed collective life' which is, for Mr Ling, the significance of the symbol of Satan in the New Testament."[1]

I would reinforce this argument with a passage from a little-known essay by the late G. K. Chesterton:

The great Huxley (on whose name be praise) said in the innocence of his heart, "It may be doubted if any man ever really said, 'Evil be thou my good.'" He could not believe that any scepticism could touch common morality, by which he really meant Christian morality. But such innocence is also ignorance. Nothing is more certain than that certain highly lucid, cultivated and deliberate men have said, "Evil, be thou my good"; men like Gilles de Rais and the Marquis de Sade. Please God they repented in the end, but the point is that they did pursue evil; not pleasure, or excess of pleasure, or sex or sensuality, but evil. And it is quite certain that some pursued it beyond the bounds of this world; and called evil forces from beyond. There is very good evidence that some of them got what they asked for.[2]

Chesterton also made the following very pertinent observation:

Common sense will show that the habit of invoking

[1] ibid., pp. 110ff.   [2] *The Common Man*, p. 95.

evil spirits, often because they were evil, has existed in far too vast a variety of different cultures, classes and social conditions to be a chance piece of childish credulity. Experience will show that it is *not* true that it disappears everywhere before the advance of education; on the contrary, some of its most evil ministers have been the most highly educated. Record will show that it is *not* true that it marks barbarism rather than civilisation; there was more devil-worship in the cities of Hannibal and Montezuma than among the Esquimaux or the Australian bushmen. And any real knowledge of modern cities will show that it is going on in London and Paris today.[1]

It is, I think, quite inadequate to dismiss belief in evil spirits as a morbid – or even as a helpful – personification of the spirit of unredeemed collective life, a kind of projection of our own social failures and frustrations on an imaginary whipping-boy. Still less can one be satisfied to substitute for it, as was popular in some circles a decade or two ago, an impersonal category of "the demonic", which was supposed to characterise the created world, a sort of built-in kink or twist which perverted all its functioning. To attribute evil to the sinful decision of beings with free-will no doubt raises many difficult problems, but to invest the created world as such with a demonic character is to blame this directly upon God the Creator. It lands us in a form of the

[1] ibid., p. 94.

Marcionite heresy, which troubled the Church in the second century and which taught that Jesus came to rescue us from the situation in which we had been placed by a possibly well-meaning but certainly incompetent creator. And both these forms of reinterpretation suffer from the grave defect that, while they can find some sort of place for talk about evil spirits, they have no place for talk about good ones. And it is indeed time that something was said about the latter, as I may appear to be following the example of the preacher from a foreign country who devoted an entire course of sermons to the subject of the Devil, under the three headings of "Who the Devil he is", "What the Devil he does" and "Why the Devil he does it".

We must firmly disabuse ourselves of two misconceptions, which have done widespread harm to religion. The first is that angels are simply the souls of departed human beings. It would be interesting to trace how this notion arose, but I do not think anyone here is likely to be a victim of it. Both Scripture and tradition have consistently seen angels as spiritual beings of an entirely different order from that of the human species. Disembodied human souls are incomplete human beings awaiting their reconstitution and glorification in the general resurrection; angels are bodiless intelligences, incandescent and transparent with the contemplation of the Trinity, except for those who have rebelled against God and changed the light that was in them into darkness, that is to say, have become devils. The second misconception, which is perhaps more insidious, arises from imagining or depicting angels by grossly misleading symbols. Again, it would be interesting to trace this process of gradual degeneration, but its final forms are quite familiar. One is what we might call the "Joshua-Reynolds cherub", the baby's head supported by a pair of tiny wings; for all its inadequacy this at least may suggest a direct and innocent gaze directed upon the face of God. The other is the "tombstone angel", the anaemic young woman in a long white robe, piously pointing with one finger to the clouds. Now it is obviously a task of extreme difficulty to find material images that will be at all adequate to represent beings that are purely spiritual, but the trouble with the two that I have just mentioned is that they do not suggest purely spiritual beings at all, but – especially in the case of the tombstone-angel – human beings of a very incomplete or debilitated type. One is led to wonder how far the artists who produced them really believed in angels at all. Mr A. C. Bridge has indeed asserted that angels have been too much even for our unconventional contemporary artists. In contrast with the Byzantine iconographers, he says, "modern painters, however good, find it impossible to make anything of angels"; they produce either lifeless imitations or decorative *motifs*, and he places in the last category the angels on the engraved glass panels in Coventry Cathedral. A living symbol, he tells us, would have challenged the beholder to belief or unbelief, but *pastiche* – mere imitation – "can only imitate or confirm incredulity".[1]

The word "incredulity" is, I suggest, the key-word here. You cannot even begin to depict angels unless you really believe in them and have some concept of their nature and functions. C. S. Lewis, who very firmly believed in them, gives in one of his novels an account, which is both instructive and amusing, of a series of attempts on the part of angels to manifest themselves in forms intelligible to a human being. The first is described as "a tornado of sheer monstrosities. . . . Darting pillars filled with eyes, lightning pulsations of flame, talons and beaks and billowy masses of what suggested snow, volleyed through cubes and heptagons into an infinite black void". And the effect upon the man Ransom was simply unbearable. In the second attempt "there came rolling wheels. There was nothing but that – concentric wheels moving with a rather sickening slowness one inside the other. There was nothing terrible about them if you could get used to their appalling size, but there was also nothing significant. He bade them to try a third time". And then there appeared two gigantic, incandescent figures in human form, compared with whose glory, at once dynamic and stable, the whole planetary environment seemed tilting and drifting. One – the angel of Mars – shone with a light that was pure, hard and bracing; the other – the angel of Venus – glowed with a warm splendour. But on the

[1] *Images of God*, pp. 28f.

faces of both one single changeless expression was stamped, which the observer could in the end only identify as charity. "But it was terrifyingly different from the expression of human charity, which we always see either blossoming out of, or descending into, natural affection. . . . Pure, spiritual, intellectual love shot from their faces like barbed lightning. It was so unlike the love we experience that its expression could easily be mistaken for ferocity."[1]

These disjointed extracts from Lewis's magnificent description do it scant justice, and he himself was keenly conscious of its inadequacy. Nevertheless, written as it was by a man who genuinely believed in what the Eastern Church strikingly calls "the holy bodiless powers", it carries with it a note of conviction and vigour which is only too rare in modern angelology. For Lewis, spirit was more, not less, substantial than matter; in *The Great Divorce* the blades of grass in the heavenly country cut the feet of the earthly visitor. He had no use for the notion of the spiritual realm as a region inhabited by filmy, drifting, amorphous wraiths. And in this I am sure he was right.

Being, as we are, composite creatures, made up of soul and body in mysterious and intimate union, it is inevitable that we should both think and speak of spiritual realities in material terms, if we are to think and speak of them at all. That the mind turns to sense-images ("phantasms") is a commonplace in Christian philosophy. If,

[1] *Perelandra* (*Voyage to Venus*), ch. xvi.

therefore, a spirit is to manifest itself to a human being, it must of necessity be represented in some visible, tangible form, and the least inadequate will probably be some human appearance of dazzling splendour. But how much of the detail is contributed by God, how much by the spirit, and how much by the human percipient is practically impossible to determine, and it does not very much matter. What does matter is whether the spiritual visitant is intent upon God's work or the devil's; this is a much more serious question and equally difficult to answer, for, as St Paul reminded his Corinthian congregation, even Satan fashions himself into an angel of light.[1] And the lives of the Saints are plentiful with stories of diabolic visitants masquerading as messengers of God. Toward these, as toward other supernormal phenomena, the Church has therefore wisely taken up an attitude of temperate scepticism, on the ground that one can perfectly well do God's will and attain eternal life by the ordinary means of grace, whereas to accept as divine a manifestation that is in fact diabolical may do untold and irreparable harm.

This point has been well made by Dr Heinrich Schlier in the following words:

Frequently there is only a thin dividing line between good and bad spirits, and it is only a clear and sharp insight which God grants us that can tell the difference, and dispel the mist which the evil spirit deliber-

[1] II Corinthians xi, 14.

ately creates. Where this gift is lacking, there is a danger that we may suspect the dark influence of the devil to be at work everywhere, so that we may never recognise him when he is really there; or we may minimise his presence and fail to see him even when he is in our midst.[1]

One fact that sometimes causes perplexity is the very much greater concern that the New Testament appears to have with evil spirits than with good ones. There are, of course, a number of individual instances of beneficent angelic appearances, the angels that brought good news to Zacharias and to Mary, the angelic choir at the Nativity, the angel in the Garden of Gethsemane, the angels at the Resurrection and the Ascension, the angel that delivered Peter from prison. But when the Epistles speak about superhuman bodiless powers, they almost invariably seem to be either definitely evil or at least highly ambiguous, "the prince of the power of the air, of the spirit that now worketh in the sons of disobedience",[2] the principalities, the powers, the virtues, the dominions[3]; all these were made by Christ[4], but the suggestion is that, subject though they are to Christ, they may be at least as much a hindrance to his work as an assistance; in the last resort they cannot separate a man from the love of God which is in Christ, but they do not seem to be actively concerned to unite him to it.[5]

[1] *Principalities and Powers in the New Testament*, p. 66.
[2] Ephesians ii, 2.   [3] Ephesians i, 21.
[4] Colossians i, 16.   [5] Ephesians i, 21; Romans viii, 38.

The answer to this problem is, I think, really quite simple. It is that, just because it is the sole purpose and aim of the good spirits to carry out the will of God, their activity cannot normally be distinguished from his; nor do they wish that it should. It is only when some specific task is allotted to them that their own individuality and operation become manifest. On the other hand, the demonic effort is one of sheer self-assertion, and in particular of self-assertion against God. It is not surprising, therefore, that the powers of darkness show themselves as a turbulent multitude of mutually conflicting egoisms. Their name is Legion, for they are many, and all that they can produce in the last resort is chaos. And, because true personality is the fruit of union with God and performance of his will, they have fallen to a level of being and action which can hardly be recognised as personal at all, a blind and obstinate determination to hate and to destroy. This, as it seems to me, is why in the New Testament the demonic powers are often spoken about more as if they were natural forces than as if they were intelligent beings. They have "lost the good of the intellect"; they have only the faceless impetus of the mob. As Schlier puts it:

The manifold principalities which unfold the one satanic power are encountered as a kind of personal and powerful being. . . . They interpret the world and existence unto death, as temptation and falsehood.

Death, sin and falsehood mark the inmost tendency of their nature, and, therefore, its fruit.

Nevertheless:

Their power has been broken on the cross and in the resurrection. Like everything else which happened there, this will be finally and completely revealed in the Second Coming of Christ Triumphant. Their defeat will then be shown to be eternal rejection. Until then, mankind and the world must suffer the ever increasing attacks of the principalities which know that they have been judged and, therefore, increase their anxious frenzy. Having no other future than eternal damnation, the principalities concentrate their attack on those who have an eternal future, namely, the Church and her members.[1]

And again Schlier writes:

The New Testament makes it clear that the onslaught of the principalities, while affecting creation generally, has now as its supreme objective Jesus Christ and his Church. The Church is the scene of the triumph of the majesty of Jesus, and in it even now – though in an obscure and symbolic fashion – justice and truth rise up in and through her members, not deriving from pride and not reflecting self-seeking. And the Church is also the realm in and through which the principalities are defeated time and again

[1] op. cit., pp. 67f.

by Jesus Christ, and where their final ruin is fore-shadowed.[1]

There has been preserved for us a precious little work from the fourth century, written by the great Bishop of Alexandria St Athanasius, the life of his friend the hermit Antony, who died at the age of one hundred and five in A.D. 356. If, as some have suggested, it is to some extent coloured by elements from the lives of other ascetics of the time, it will be all the more valuable as an account of the monastic ideal, but this is doubtful. One thing stands out quite plainly, that Antony as he is here depicted was certainly not fleeing into solitude from human society in order to engage in the peaceful and uneventful cultivation of his own soul. To a straight-forward and simple Egyptian mind it seemed that, in the great cities where the Church was established and the sacraments constantly celebrated, the devil must have been already expelled and his power almost des-troyed, though from what we know about Alexandria at the time this may seem to be a somewhat roseate estimate of its condition. And it seemed to Antony that the devil had been driven from the haunts of men and had presumably taken refuge in the desert.[2] So Antony, like his Master Christ, went out to meet Satan in the wilderness; and there, without any doubt, he found him. As we have already seen, the spiritual powers,

[1] ibid., p. 52.
[2] Cf. L. Bouyer, *La Vie de S. Antoine*, p. 101.

whether good or bad, appear to men in the forms which their minds suggest and which they can understand; and so it was with Antony. I shall not weary you with details of the assaults which he underwent except to mention that they largely consisted of sheer brute physical violence and that they were rather less volupt-uous than Gustave Flaubert and the painters have con-ceived them. The point which I want to make is that Antony's lifelong determination was to assist in mop-ping up the already routed powers of evil, and he never wavered in his conviction that it was he and not the devil that was on the winning side. Thus, when he felt himself assailed by a great host of demons, he met them with ridicule: So many demons to one poor monk! "If you had any power, one of you would be sufficient. But Christ has hamstrung you, and so you try to frighten me by your numbers." The weapons at Antony's disposal it is true, were spiritual ones; hence the long years of solitude, prayer and fasting. But the purpose was not, as it might have been with many oriental ascetics, simply the personal beatitude of Antony; it was the defeat of those powers which, in Schlier's words, now have as the supreme objective of their onslaught the Church and her members. And so it has always been in the religious life, when it has been vigorous and healthy. Nothing could be further from the truth than the idea that it is self-centred or motivated by disgust for God's creation; and when a Christian writer speaks of con-tempt of the world, he is using the word "world" not to mean God's creation or human life as such, but, as the New Testament often uses it, to signify the organisation of human life in opposition to, or in neglect of, the God in whose will alone man can find lasting happiness and peace.

You may perhaps feel that some apology is due for the fact that this lecture has been devoted almost entirely to the warfare in the unseen realm, about which most Christians today rarely think and which many would dismiss as at best picturesque myth and at worst pure fiction. It is for this very reason that it has seemed to me urgent to emphasise it. Scripture, tradition and Christian experience combine in assuring us that the struggle against evil with which Christians on earth are concerned can be seen in its true proportions only against the background of a vaster and more mysterious conflict in the unseen world in which they too are caught up. When we are faced with the claim that Christians in a secular age ought to live as completely secularised men we can only reply that such a programme does no justice either to the true nature of this world or of existence as a whole, and that it totally misunderstand the nature of the forces with which we are opposed. It ignores also the resources which we have at our command. It is related in the Second Book of the Kings that, on waking one morning, the prophet Elisha discovered that the city in which he was had been invested by an armed host. "His servant said unto him, 'Alas, my master, how shall we do?' And he answered,

I

'Fear not; for they that be with us are more than they that be with them.' And Elisha prayed and said, 'Lord, I pray thee, open his eyes that he may see.' And the Lord opened the eyes of the young man, and he saw. And behold, the mountain was full of horses and chariots of fire round about Elisha."[1]

[1] II Kings vi, 15–17.

CHAPTER SEVEN

All Things in Christ

AFTER OUR CONDUCTED TOUR THROUGH THE realms of the angels and the devils it will be well for us to return to the main road and continue our journey. I hope, however, that we shall not allow ourselves to forget that greater warfare in the heavenly places, against the background of which all our earthly struggles are fought. For, although it is a background, it is more than a background; it is a conflict into which we ourselves are drawn, since God's creation is not sealed off into airtight compartments. The Prayer Book collect for the Feast of St. Michael and all Angels begins by proclaiming that God has constituted the services of angels and men in a wonderful order (not, we must observe, in *two* wonderful orders), and therefore prays that, as his holy angels always do him service in heaven, so by his appointment they may succour and defend us on earth.

But to continue with our main theme. That theme, you will remember, is twofold. First it maintains that, while the world and human life do not make sense of themselves, God makes sense of them, since it is by him and in him and for him that they exist. Secondly, it maintains that God the Son, the Second Person of the Eternal Trinity, has united human nature to himself –

has, as we say, "become man" – in order that both the human race and the material universe, of which the human race is part, may be taken up into the very life of God himself and be transformed into a condition of unimaginable splendour.

We must now remind ourselves that this transformation of the human race and this glorification of the material universe have already begun. There are three misconceptions to be avoided here. The first is that, while the individual figure in human history, Jesus of Nazareth, is perfect man, the one person in all history who has lived in all respects as human beings are meant to live, all other human beings, are, so to speak, simply outside him; that he has done great things for them, they have received great benefits from him, they can be inspired by his example and instructed by his teaching, but they are not in any true sense sharers in his life. The second misconception is this: that certain men and women have been brought into a genuine and intimate relation to Jesus Christ, but the rest of the human race is in the same condition as that in which it would be if he had never appeared on this earth at all. This misconception can take several forms: it can limit the privileged élite either to those who have been chosen by an arbitrary decision on the part of God, or to those who have been justified by making an act of faith in Christ, or to those who have been baptised into the sacramental body of the Church, or to those who hold certain specified beliefs, or to those who belong to a particular religious organisation; but all forms of it restrict the benefits of the Incarnation to one small portion of mankind. The third misconception is this: that Jesus Christ is of immense significance to human beings, but of no importance whatever to the rest of the universe. This last view is very common today. It interprets Christianity entirely in terms of personal relationships between human beings; it sees great significance in the fact that we are members of the human community but none in the fact that, in our bodily aspect, we are physical objects, parts of the material world.

Now the reason why all these misconceptions are so harmful is that each of them contains a large element of truth. Sheer and absolute falsehoods are comparatively rare, and, however reprehensible they may be in themselves, they usually do little harm, for their falsity is generally obvious. It is the half-truths that are really pernicious, for the truth that is in them can delude people into swallowing them whole. And so it is here. Jesus Christ is indeed unique in human history; he is the only man who is also God, he alone is the redeemer of the world. Even those Christians who hold that the Mother of Jesus was immaculately conceived and free from all sin, both original and actual, insist, as the Second Vatican Council has made quite plain[1], that she is altogether secondary and subordinate to him. Again, it matters a great deal that a man should have faith in Christ, and that he should be baptised into the

[1] *Dogmatic Constitution on the Church*, para. 62.

Church and that he should live as a convinced and active member of it. It also matters a great deal that a man is a man, and not an octopus or a parsnip or a lump of bauxite. But this does not mean that the effect of God having become man in Jesus is confined either to Jesus himself, or to Christians or even to the human race; it simply means that the various orders of being are affected by it in different ways. And, since our human minds find it difficult to think of anything without employing images and illustrations that are derived from the realm of material objects, may I put before you a very simple picture consisting of four circles, of different sizes, all lying in the same plane and all having the same centre.

The innermost circle will represent Jesus of Nazareth himself, the man who walked and taught in Palestine and was crucified under Pontius Pilate, who rose from the dead in majesty and glory and who, in his ascension, removed himself from human sight and touch, though not from human existence. At the centre of this circle is the Person of God the Son, who is the subject of all these human experiences and activities. This Divine Person must be represented in our diagram simply by a point, for otherwise we should have to remove part of the innermost circle to make room for it, and this would be to make Jesus something less than fully man. But we must not think that because in our diagram the Divine Person is represented merely by a point – by something which, as Euclid would say, has position but not magnitude – it is therefore less real than the circle of which it is the centre; it is in fact far more real. In order to conceive its full status we must get out of our flat two-dimensional diagram altogether into the third dimension; and then we shall see that the Divine Person infinitely surpasses the flat diagram in every respect. The point-centre of the circle is, so to speak, the place where the Divine Person intersects it; it is the place where he is the subject of his human nature. It is also the place where the Divine Person holds the whole diagram together; in the words of the Epistle to the Colossians, "all things are held together in him."[1] But this will become clearer when we see what the other circles stand for.

The second circle, counting outwards from the centre, will represent the Body of Christ which is the Church; that is to say, the organic totality of men and women who, by faith and baptism, are visibly incorporated into Jesus and whose union with him is maintained and increased by prayer and the sacraments. The third circle will represent the whole human race. And the fourth and outermost circle will stand for the whole of the physical universe. The space outside that may perhaps designate the realm of the angels, the "holy bodiless powers".

Now it goes without saying that every model or diagram of this kind has its limitations, and if it is pressed too far it will lead us into heresy or absurdity. Nevertheless, this one has its uses, and I think we can

[1] Colossians i. 17.

develop it a little further, while drawing attention to its dangers as we come to them.

First, then, each of the four circles includes those that are inside it. This does not apply to the space outside the fourth circle; the angels no doubt envelop the material creation with their beneficent (or, in the case of the fallen angels, maleficent) activity, but they do not include it as part of themselves. The material creation (the fourth circle) does, however, include the human race; as I remarked in an earlier lecture, we are material beings that can only keep alive by stuffing material objects into holes at one end of us. But – and here is the first of the danger-signals – we are not *purely* material beings. We are made of matter and spirit intimately and mysteriously united; the diagram therefore expresses only part of the truth about us. Again, the human race (the third circle) includes the Church. But here we had better remind ourselves that, if Christianity is true, neither the Church nor the human race is confined to this world; the greater part of both is beyond the grave, and a great deal of both has not yet come into existence. Finally, Jesus himself (the first circle) is a member of both the Church and the human race, though he is, of course, a quite special and unique member of both. All history before his appearance converges upon him, and all subsequent human history fans out from him. In St Paul's phrase, he is the "Second Adam", the man from whom the human race begins again and in whom it is all summed up. He is the heir – the "firstborn" – of all creation, and he is the Head of the Body, the Church[1]. God "put all things in subjection under his feet, and gave him to be Head over all things to the Church, which is his Body, the fullness of him that filleth all in all."[2]

With the cautions mentioned, then, each circle includes those inside it. Mankind is part of the material creation, the Church is part of mankind, Jesus himself is a member – although the Head – of the Church and therefore of the human race. But simply because at the very centre of the manhood of Jesus, and so of the whole diagram, there is to be found something that is not a creature at all, but the uncreated Person of God the Son, "through whom all things were made"[3] we see that this inward movement of inclusion expresses only one side of the truth. When we get to the very heart of the created world, we find the uncreated Creator himself, present in his creative power throughout the world's existence, and present as man since the day when the Angel of the Lord brought the tidings to Mary.

Secondly, although the circles mark out definite realms, they must not be thought of as impermeable membranes. Christ's manhood does not cut him off from the Church; rather it is the source from which grace pours into the Church and fills it with life and power. Again, the Church is not sealed off from the world; although, from one point of view, it consists, like

[1] Colossians i, 18.   [2] Ephesians i, 22, 23.
[3] Nicene Creed, echoing John i, 3.

the ark of Noah, of those who have been saved by baptism from the flood of a sinful world[1], it is also the leaven by which the whole mass of the world is to be leavened and the light that is to lighten the whole world. [2] And indeed in the providence of God the circle of the Church is to enlarge itself more and more, as it embraces more and more of mankind. Nor, again, is there an impassable boundary between mankind and the material creation; there is, of course, no question of the lower creation becoming *part* of mankind, as human beings can and do become members of the Church; but it is by subserving the material welfare of mankind that the material realm fulfils its highest function and reaches its highest end. What greater function have bread and fish ever exercised than to be the food eaten by Jesus of Nazareth? What greater function do bread and wine exercise today than to become the Eucharistic body which is the food of his Mystical Body the Church? And this Eucharistic use of bread and wine is only the summit and the symbol of the use, by man redeemed in Christ, of the material creatures which God has provided for man's sustenance, and of the transformation of all things in Christ.

There is thus, as it were, a radiation of grace from the centre to the circumference, from the Divine Person of Christ to his manhood, from Christ's manhood to his Church, from the Church to the human race, from the human race to the material universe, out to that ex-

[1] I Peter iii, 20, 21.   [2] Matthew xiii, 33; v, 14.

treme limit where the material universe itself impinges in action and reaction upon the holy bodiless powers.

If something like this is true – and I would remind you again of the inadequacy of all pictorial representations of the mysteries of God – we are, I would suggest, called to a radical reorientation of our outlook upon both the Church and the world. Under the stresses and turmoils of the Church's history men have come to look upon the Church, in its more prosperous phrases, as a victorious army making war against unbelievers or, in its darker days, as a besieged castle in which the faithful who are fortunate enough to be inside may hope to resist the assaults of the enemy without. Now I do not want to deny the legitimacy of martial imagery in Christian speaking and writing; the New Testament is well supplied with it. But we must remember that the warfare in which the Christian is engaged *as a Christian* is not against other men but against the powers of darkness: "our wrestling is not against flesh and blood, but against the principalities, against the powers, against the world-rulers of this darkness, against the spiritual hosts of wickedness in the heavenly places."[1] "God sent not his Son into the world to judge the world, but that the world should be saved through him."[2] Christ's warfare is fought not *against* man, but *in* man and *for* man. And the grace which comes from Christ to his Church flows also from the Church into the whole human race. To say this is not in the least degree to render the

[1] Ephesians vi, 12.   [2] John iii, 17.

Church unnecessary or membership of it optional; on the contrary, it is to stress the fact that there are things – the most vital things of all – that the Church does for the world which the world cannot do for itself. And this is all the more important at a time when so many of the tasks which the Church did for the world when the world had not learnt to do them for itself are now being done by the world very successfully – education, medical care and the rest of the social services. The one thing that the Church can do for the world which the world will never be able to do for itself, at least until the kingdoms of this world have themselves become the kingdom of God and of his Christ, is to offer the world to God to be transfigured by his grace and to be taken into his life.

May I quote to you the following words from a Roman Catholic writer who has seen this with remarkable clarity:

The particular strength, then, of the modern insights in theology [he is speaking primarily of insights in his own Church] is this existential stress upon the personal approach. The Godhead itself is seen as a dramatic dialogue between Father and Son issuing in the Holy Ghost. God's saving action in the world is the outcome of this conversation pursued outside the confines of the Trinity. While on earth the Body of Christ responds with its own divinely given communication, which is the Liturgy. No wonder that the notable mark of the Church in this decade is this sudden urge to speak to all men, "to enter into dialogue with the modern world".

And for this very reason – just because we have to speak as men to men – Fr John Dalrymple stresses the necessity of the Liturgy and of prayer.

We Christians know that the only person who can release a man from the bondage of selfhood and draw him out of himself is Christ. The question is whether we today offer Christ to the world as a liberating person, or as an agent of restriction. If we are to show forth Christ as a liberating agent then we must first have entered into that liberation ourselves; we must first have conquered our primal fears; we must first have prayed.[1]

Let us come back to our diagram, with the Incarnate Son of God at the centre, surrounded by the successive circles of Church, man, and the material world, suffused and vivified by the grace that flows from the centre to the circumference. And with that in mind, may I read you the following passage from the Vatican Decree on the Liturgy:

Christ Jesus, High Priest of the New and Eternal Covenant, taking human nature, introduced into this earthly exile that hymn which is sung throughout all ages in the halls of heaven. He joins the entire com-

[1] *Blackfriars*, XLVI (1965), pp. 575f.

munity of mankind to himself, associating it with his own singing of this canticle of divine praise.

For he continues his priestly work through the agency of his Church, which is ceaselessly engaged in praising the Lord and interceding for the salvation of the whole world. She does this, not only by celebrating the Eucharist, but also in other ways, especially by praying the Divine Office. . . .

Therefore when this wonderful song of praise is duly performed by priests and others who are deputed for the purpose by the Church's ordinance, or when the faithful pray together with the priest in the approved form, then it is truly the voice of the Bride addressed to her Bridegroom; it is the very prayer which Christ himself, together with his Body, offers to the Father.

Hence all who render this service are not only fulfilling a duty of the Church, but are also sharing in the greatest honour of Christ's spouse, for by duly offering these praises to God they are standing before God's throne in the name of their Mother the Church.[1]

What a tremendous conception this is! Christ, by becoming man, has caught up the whole human race into the act of praise which, in the life of the Holy Trinity, he eternally offers to the glory of God the

[1] *Constitution on the Liturgy*, paras. 83–85, trans. Clifford Howell, S.J.

Father, and his Church and its members are the lips
through which he utters that act of praise on earth. Nor
is this great act of offering which is the Church's
privilege confined to the Liturgy itself. When Christ's
members take their various parts in the activities of
mankind they are functioning as members of the Body
which the Liturgy perpetuates and sustains. They are
the agents of the Christification of the universe, and it
is in the light of this fact that their secular activities are
to be assessed and judged. In spite of his odd use of
words and his occasional lack of precision, Teilhard de
Chardin seems to have grasped this truth more firmly
and jubilantly than any of our contemporaries. His
meditation entitled "The Mass on the World", composed on the Feast of the Transfiguration when, in the
Chinese desert, he was unable to celebrate Mass but
was inspired by the recognition that his work as a
palaeontologist, no less than his priesthood, was a share
in the Christification of the universe, is perhaps the most
moving expression that he ever gave to it. It does not
lend itself to fragmentary quotation, so may I read to
you some short passages from another work of his, *Le
Milieu Divin*.

As a consequence of the Incarnation, the divine im-
mensity has transformed itself for us into *the omni-
presence of christification*. All the good that I can do . . .
is physically gathered in, by something of itself, into
the reality of the consummated Christ. Everything I

endure, with faith and love, by way of diminishment or death, makes me a little more closely an integral part of his mystical body. Quite specifically it is *Christ whom we make or whom we undergo in all things*. Not only are all things turned into good for those who love, but, more clearly still, they are turned into God and, quite explicitly, they are turned into Christ.

And, again:

When the priest says the words "This is my body", his words fall directly on to the bread and directly transform it into the individual reality of Christ. But the great sacramental operation does not cease at that local and momentary event. Even children are taught that, throughout the life of each man and the life of the Church and the history of the world, there is only one Mass and one Communion. Christ died once in agony. Peter and Paul receive communion on such and such a day at a particular hour. But these different acts are only the diversely central points in which the continuity of a unique act is split up and fixed, in space and time, for our experience. In fact, from the beginning of the Messianic preparation, up till the Parousia [the return of Christ in glory], passing through the historic manifestation of Jesus and the phases of growth of his Church, a single event has been developing in the world: the Incarnation, realised, in each individual, through the Eucharist.

And the third passage:

Around the earth, the centre of our field of vision, the souls of men form, in some manner, the incandescent surface of matter plunged in God. From the dynamic and biological point of view it is quite as impossible to draw a line below it, as to draw a line between a plant and the environment that sustains it. If, then, the Eucharist is a sovereign influence upon our human natures, then its energy necessarily extends, owing to the effects of continuity, into the less luminous regions that sustain us. . . . At every moment the Eucharistic Christ controls – from the point of view of the organisation of the Pleroma [the final fulfilment] (which is the only true point of view from which the world can be understood) – the whole movement of the universe: the Christ "through whom, O Lord, thou dost ever create, quicken and bestow on us all things."[1]

Now at this point we may very naturally find ourselves reflecting that, if this great vision of the gathering of the universe into Christ is true, it is more difficult than ever to believe in the doctrine of hell, that is to say to believe that, in spite of the fact that Christ died for the salvation of the whole of mankind and that it is God's will that all men should be saved, it is nevertheless possible for a human being to refuse that salvation

[1] *Le Milieu Divin*, pp. 112–115. Latin phrases translated into English and comments in [ ] added by the present author. The final words are quoted from the canon of the Roman Mass.

K

and in consequence to condemn himself to an eternity of self-frustration and misery. (Note the word "possible"; the Church has never allowed us to say that any human being – not Judas or Gilles de Rais or Himmler – has in the critical moment made that terrible refusal, and I am sure that Dante himself would have expected to find at the day of judgment that his own census of hell was wildly inaccurate.) How can a God of love allow any of his creatures to suffer unending misery? And how can we say that a universe in which this has happened is gathered in its entirety into Christ?

I have no slick answers to give you, but to the first question it must be replied that, so far from the fact that God is love making hell impossible, the fact that God is love makes hell necessary. If all that God was prepared to confer on us was a state of impersonal or merely animal beatitude, he might easily give it to us all, quite regardless of our attitude to him or to our fellow-creatures; the heavenly mescaline, like earthly mescaline, would produce its effects on saints and sinners, on the repentant and the defiant alike. Or if God was impersonal he could be the heavenly mescaline himself – though in this case we ought to say "itself" rather than "himself". But if God is Trinity of Persons and we are persons, and if what he has made us for and what he offers us is nothing less than life in him and with him, then we cannot have the gift unless we are prepared to accept it, and to accept it for what it is, namely the life of the creative and omnipotent Lover, on whose free bounty our very existence already depends. Union – real union, not an uneasy and unstable *modus vivendi* – by its very nature requires free and irrevocable choice on both sides; this is, incidentally, why free mutual consent is necessary for a valid marriage. And it is such a choice that confronts us, when, at the moment of death, we come into the sheer presence of God himself, as created spirits face to face with uncreated Spirit. It is no longer, as in this life, a choice between lesser goods and greater, it is no longer a choice between using God's gifts as we want to use them and using them as he wants us to use them, it is no longer a choice between serving our neighbours as we want to serve them and serving them as God wants us to serve them, it is no longer even a choice between God and creatures; it is simply a choice between accepting God and rejecting him. We can either throw ourselves in an ecstasy of adoration and gratitude into the arms of self-existent Love and find therein all the goodness and joy that we have known in this life and an infinity besides, or we can repel it in a brutish and ridiculous attempt to affirm our own self-sufficiency and be left for all eternity with nothing but our own resentful and self-lacerating selves. Such a choice has little in common with even the most critical moral choices that confront us in this life, though all of these contain a trace and a foreshadowing of it. But we cannot ignore it without implicitly denying either that God has made us for life in him or else that we are persons with free-will. Hell, as Christianity conceives it, is not incompatible with God's love; it is a direct consequence of it. For love can be received only in a free response of love; and, God's Love being pure self-giving, we must receive it as such or not at all. We cannot, by the nature of the case, have it on our own terms. We can only have it on his, for those are the expression of his nature and ours, and love cannot subsist on falsehood. If it is suggested that God will surely give us an indefinite number of second chances, the answer is very simple. It is that this is precisely what he is continually doing while we are in this life, but, when at death we see him in the fullness of his glory and love, he is giving us all the conceivable and possible chances at once. What further inducement can he set before us to win our love if the vision of his own being has been insufficient? What – if we may say it reverently – what further cards can he possibly have to play? We may indeed find it difficult to imagine that anyone whom we know or of whom we have heard will *in fact* reject God under these conditions; but in order to recognise the *possibility*, we have only to reflect on the nature of God and man and love, or, better still, to look into our own souls. The catastrophic effect of such a repudiation of God on the soul that makes it is indeed hard to picture and horrible to contemplate; it is the corruption of the will by a lie in the intellect, the obstinate attempt by a creature to live as if it were God. It is a deliberate placing of the human soul outside the human race by its own decision; and it makes the soul akin to the fallen angels. In Dante's terrible phrase, the damned are those who "have lost the good of the intellect". The soldier in Bernard Shaw's *St Joan*, who described hell as like being always drunk without having the trouble, well described the bestial torpor of the damned but failed to stress the sheer inhuman horror of these "beings that once were men".

If anything like this – and it is the traditional teaching of the Christian Church – is true, we can perhaps see the beginnings of an answer to the second problem, namely how we can say that a universe in which there will be creatures, whether men or devils, who are permanently alienated from God will have been gathered in its entirety into Christ. The point is that the damned have, by their own decision, put themselves into a condition in which the redeemed human race and the transformed, Christified order of being are simply irrelevant to them. Once again, we must not think of them as we think of even the most degraded or presumptuous of sinners in this life, the most squalidly sensual, the most self-centred, the most cruel, or the most conceited and proud. All these are still on the nearer side of the final decision, not beyond it; and as long as there are any such the ultimate membership of the redeemed community is undecided. But this state of affairs, which is characteristic of both the Church and the whole human race in this life, a state in which most of us have, so to speak, one leg firmly in the kingdom of God and the other as firmly outside it, cannot go on for all eternity. To use Christ's own illustrations, the good and the bad fish will be sorted out when the net is drawn to land, the wheat and the tares will be separated at the harvest, the guest without the wedding-robe will be thrust into outer darkness. And I think this image of darkness is very significant, for it means that the damned will be so completely excluded from the redeemed community and the realm of transfiguration that they will simply be no longer visible; they will just have ceased to count. What place could there be in any case, in a community transfused and throbbing with love, for beings that are concerned only to assert themselves? The damned will not be a kind of helot or outcaste section of the redeemed community, punished by being made to do degrading but necessary jobs for the benefit of the saved; by their own decision, their own rejection of love, they will have placed themselves outside the community altogether.

Finally, I must say a word about the problem of evil in its widest sense, as it presents itself to many people today. However glorious the final condition may be, they will say, nothing can make up for the horrors of Buchenwald or Belsen, to mention only two of the cases that come most readily to our minds. I cannot attempt in the time that remains to do more than point in the direction along which I suggest any attempts to find an answer should be directed. For a really profound discussion I would recommend Dr A. M. Farrer's remarkable book *Love Almighty and Ills Unlimited*, though I must add that I feel sure one must take the powers of darkness more seriously than he takes them. (Fortunately, the chapter "Adam and Lucifer" is not really central to his argument.) One thing at least we must not do, and that is to try to make out that evil is not really as bad as it appears to be or that it is really only good in disguise; to do this is the perennial temptation of philosophers who discuss the problem, and one is sometime led to wonder how much real evil they have encountered. The one point I wish to make is this, that it is not the mere existence of evil that makes it difficult to believe in God; otherwise, people would find it difficult to believe in God because of the discomfort involved in rowing in the Boat Race, and this does not seem to be the case. What does worry us is the occurrence of evil on a scale so great or intense that we cannot imagine anything that would ultimately compensate for it. The varsity stroke or even the patient in the dentist's waiting room has little difficulty in envisaging a situation in which his present suffering will be seen to have been not worth while bothering about. We feel very much more difficulty in envisaging a situation in which we should honestly be able to feel like that about Belsen, or babies dying of cancer, or a dozen other horrors that spring to the mind. Even God, we feel, couldn't make those not matter. Now, without in the least degree minimising these evils, I suggest that this very natural reaction is due not only to a vivid and praiseworthy sensitivity to the human situation but also to the intrinsic limitations of our human imaginations. I can imagine what will make the sufferings of the Cambridge stroke ultimately not matter, namely getting to Mortlake Brewery before the Oxford boat. I can imagine what will make my tooth-ache ultimately not matter, namely my power to forget minor agonies and not let my outlook on life become warped by them. But I cannot *imagine* how even God could produce a situation in which I could say "I now see that even Belsen doesn't really matter". However, let us approach the problem from the other end. Sup-pose – just suppose – that God's resources are so much beyond all that I can imagine that he can ultimately produce a situation in which I could honestly say "I now see that even Belsen doesn't matter, and that this is why he didn't do what I should have done if I had had the power, namely strike the Nazis all dead in order to prevent it." *If* this is true – I stress the "*if*" – then God's resources must be inexpressibly ampler that any-thing I am able to conceive. I shall leave you to develop this line of thought for yourselves, only remarking that there is some support for it in Christ's own teaching. "A woman when she is in travail hath sorrow, because her hour is come; but as soon as she is delivered of the child she remembereth no more the anguish, for joy that a man is born into the world." [1] May I add St Paul's words: "The whole creation groaneth and travaileth in pain together until now, . . . waiting for the adoption, to wit the redemption of our body." [2]

[1] John xvi, 21.   [2] Romans viii, 25.

These brief remarks do not, of course, provide a solution to the problem of evil, but they indicate the direction in which, I believe, the solution is to be sought. Our basic difficulty is that we have far too small a concept of God. In Ibsen's *Peer Gynt*, the button-maker asserted that "the Master [that is, God] . . . is economical, you see, and therefore is a man of substance."[1] This I believe to be the precise opposite of the truth. As Mr Denys Munby has written, "In heaven no problem of scarcity arises, and in hell no possibility of choice exists; economics is a science dealing with the conditions of human life in this world."[2]

God is so rich that his resources are unlimited, and we can set no bounds to either his prodigality or his power.

[1] Act V, scene ii.   [2] *Christianity and Economic Problems*, p. 44.

CHAPTER EIGHT

Task and Resources

AS I COME TO THE END OF THIS COURSE OF
lectures I am very conscious of the large number of questions connected with our subject to which I have been able to devote little or no attention. In particular, the brief remarks which I made at the end of the last lecture about the problem of evil are far too brief to be adequate. Nevertheless, rather than pile inadequacy upon inadequacy I shall merely recommend to you two books which seem to me to take us as far into the heart of this deep and terrible mystery as it is possible for the minds of men to go. One, which I mentioned in the last lecture, is Dr Farrer's *Love Almighty and Ills Unlimited*; the other is C. S. Lewis's *Problem of Pain*. There is, however, one point which I would stress: that, interesting as it is from the academic standpoint to enquire for an explanation of the existence of evil, the really important question is what, if anything, we can *do* about it. And here we have the witness, not only of great Christian thinkers and mystics but of myriads of simple Christian men and women, that that particular form of evil which we know as pain, both mental and physical, can, if it is offered to God by the sufferer in union with the suffering and death of Christ, be *used* as a positive

means for the destruction of evil itself. Indeed, such is the coinherence of the human race and the Church in Christ that it would seem that the final triumph of God over evil, in which will be fulfilled the prophet's words "He shall look upon the travail of his soul and be satisfied",[1] will include among the means by which it has been brought about the redemptive sufferings of Christ's members. "I fill up," wrote St Paul, "that which is lacking in the afflictions of Christ in my flesh for his body's sake which is the Church."[2] As the Abbé Nédoncelle has written, "Christianity has done something better than expound the nature of evil: it has provided mankind with a ferment which dissolves it."[3] And on this deep level of coinherence and identification I know nothing profounder than Gerard Manley Hopkins's poem "The Wreck of the Deutschland", which has been so brilliantly interpreted for us by Canon Philip Martin in his *Mastery and Mercy*.

I propose, however, now to leave this great mystery and to devote this lecture to the thoroughly straightforward and down-to-earth question of the way in which a Christian should think and live in this secularised world if he is to be true to his Christian vocation. And in the first place I suggest he must constantly remind himself of the supreme reality of God and of Christ. May I quote to you three passages to this effect, all, as it happens, written by laypeople. The first is from

[1] Isaiah liii, 11.
[2] Colossians i, 24.   [3] *Baron Friedrich von Hügel*, p. 120

Mr A. H. Hodges, Professor of Philosophy at Reading University:

> He [that is, God] is our King. His claims over us are unlimited and unconditional. He claims every aspect of our being and activity, in every place and at every moment, from the hour of our birth to the utmost reaches of eternity. And in all this he seems not to be making demands on us, but to be satisfying our deepest desires; for he has fashioned us so that only in this complete and unconditional surrender to him can our own happiness be found.[1]

My second quotation is from Mr Hugo Meynell:

> That Jesus Christ is true God and true man entails that our ultimate fate is determined by our relationship to him; that all of our other relationships in this world and the next, and everything that can possibly happen to us, are in comparison of no importance whatever.[2]

And the third passage is from Miss Barbara Reynolds's Introduction to the *Paradiso* of Dante:

> It is in the *Paradiso* that we find affirmed with the utmost clarity and consistency the fundamental Christian proposition that the journey to God is the journey into reality. To know all things in God is to know them as they really are, for God is the only

---

[1] *The Way of Integration*, p. 15.
[2] *Sense, Nonsense and Christianity*, p. 232.

absolute and unconditioned Reality, of whose being all contingent realities are at best the types and mirrors, at worst the shadows and distortions – at best the created universe, at worse the deliberately willed delusion which we call Hell.[1]

Now to maintain in one's mind this sense of the utter reality and primacy of God and of his claims upon us is – let us admit it frankly – an extremely exacting task in the world in which we live. For we are surrounded by techniques of mass suggestion, designed with the utmost skill at vast expense by people who have things to sell, and all based on the assumption that the ends worth pursuing in life are money, social prestige, positions of influence, and success with the opposite sex, appealing, that is to say, to covetousness, pride, the desire for power, ambition and lust. It is an instructive and a sobering way of spending ten minutes to look at the advertisements in a newspaper or on the walls of an Underground station and ask yourself in each case to which of your impulses it is addressed. And I think you will find yourself saying, with the late William George Peck, "If I'm the sort of being that the man who designed those advertisements thinks I am, then I'm not the sort of being the Gospel thinks I am." To show how Satan can transform himself into an angel of light and deceive the very elect, may I quote from a leaflet circulated to advertisers in the United States by a journal

[1] *The Divine Comedy* (Penguin Classics edition), III, p. 16.

describing itself as "the officially sponsored independ-
ently-edited national magazine for all Episcopalians"
and as having "the largest circulation ever achieved by
any national consumer-religious magazine":

> Pin down your share of this multi-million dollar
> market! Get the facts about this responsive prestige
> market. Write for brochure which outlines educa-
> tional levels, income brackets, home and car owner-
> ship and many other vital marketing statistics.
> EPISCOPAL FAMILIES *have* MORE AND THEY *spend*
> MORE![1]

("Episcopal families", of course, does not mean the
families of bishops, but of Episcopalians, or, as we
should say, of Anglicans.) This is, needless to say, such
a crude and blatant example that only a very insensitive
Churchman could fail to be revolted by it, but it is
worth asking ourselves how far we ourselves have become unconsciously indoctrinated by the scale of values
which it presupposes. If we are to maintain, not only in
our vocal declarations but, what is far more important,
in our subconscious assumptions, the primacy of God
over our lives and the fact that life in God is the end for
which we are made, we must develop the habit of ques-
tioning incessantly the scale of values which underlies
not only the advertisements – though it is perhaps most
obvious in them – but also a great deal of the other

[1] Quoted in *Anglican Digest*, Autumn 1963, which was not the
journal in question.

material which is offered to our eyes and ears in newspapers, books, films, sound-broadcasting and television.

Nevertheless – and this is equally important – to recognise the primacy and supremacy of God does not mean to treat God's creatures as in themselves contemptible or valueless. It means, on the contrary, to rescue them from the degradation to which they are commonly subjected and to assist them to achieve the end for which God has made them. As we saw in an earlier lecture, God's purpose for the human race and for the universe of which it is part is that they should be transfigured in Christ and his body the Church. Thus, while we must resist with all our power, the *secularising of theology* – that is to say, the reduction of the Christian religion to a concern simply with the things of this world and our life on this planet – we must do all in our power to work out, both in theory and in practice, a *theology of the secular* – that is to say, an outlook which sees the things of this world and of our earthly life as redeemed by Christ and destined ultimately to find their place in the final transfiguration of all things in him; what the French call *une théologie des réalités terrestres*, a theology of earthly realities. If we fail to do this, we cannot be surprised if the secular realm arrogates to itself a demonic autonomy, a self-sufficiency which is a diabolic parody of the sovereignty of God. If, on the other hand, we see the world in terms of this theology of the secular, we shall also be able to see all the activities of human beings, except those that are inherently sinful, as contributing to the final consummation. We shall see man as nature's priest, in whose work and by whose hands God's world is offered to him to be transformed by his acceptance of it. And here there are several points that need to be stressed.

In the first place, if we are to avoid romanticism and sentimentality, we must recognise that while there are some jobs which it is easy to see as "offerable" to God, there are others, equally necessary, whose offerability is less immediately apparent. The work of a university teacher and researcher, for example, fairly clearly falls into the former category, in spite of the drudgery involved in the occasional marking of some hundreds of examination papers or the boredom of many academic committees. On the other hand, while a saint can make the cleaning of a sewer or the adding up of endless columns of figures a direct means of glorifying God, the *homme moyen sensuel*, the "ordinary chap", can hardly be expected to see it as more than an unpleasant but necessary job by which he earns his living. This means that, although the work of the human race as a whole, where it is not positively sinful or aimless, glorifies God as it helps the world towards its final consummation, the parts that are played by individual men and women often have little meaning in isolation and only acquire significance as parts of the whole. For this theological reason – the destination of the human race to its ultimate transfiguration – and not only on grounds of social expediency and justice, society has a special duty to those of its members whose jobs are constricting, drab or dangerous, to provide them with opportunities for the constructive and fulfilling use of their leisure. However, this whole situation will rapidly become one of the past if, without economic chaos or nuclear catastrophe, we pass smoothly into an epoch in which technological development and automation provide the great mass of the population with almost unlimited leisure. Freed for the first time in human history from the need of exhausting labour to keep himself alive, man will have a greater opportunity than ever before to transfigure for the glory of God both his own life and the world of which he is part. Needless to say, with these new possibilities of good there will be new possibilities for evil, for the range within which man can exercise his freedom to choose and to plan will be vastly enlarged. The example of those privileged people whose wealth has exempted them from the need of working for their living does not suggest that leisure in itself is always productive of benefits for the community as a whole. Satan finds some mischief still for idle hands to do, and it cannot be said of all the leisured as it is of Mr Granville Sharp on his monument in Westminster Abbey that

Freed by competence from the necessity and by content
　　from the desire
　　　　　　Of lucrative occupation
He was incessant in his labour to improve the condition
　　of mankind
　　　　Founding public happiness on private virtue.

L

This is not the place to attempt the solution of these problems or even to forecast what their precise nature will be; it will require the intelligent and humble co-operation of experts in every sphere and on every plane. What is urgent is that Christians shall not be taken unawares by either the opportunities or the pitfalls of the situation; we may well heed Berdyaev's cutting observation that "one of the greatest tragedies of Christians is that they are always too late"[1]. And if the Christian religion is true, the basic fact is that man, in both his work and his leisure (if, indeed, it will be possible in the future to distinguish between the two), is called, as nature's priest, to be God's agent and vice-gerent in what Teilhard de Chardin described in his pregnant phrase as the "Christification" of the world.

But what, we may ask, in this process is the place of the Church as such? Much, every way. First, it is the Church's duty to proclaim, in season and out of season, that the world is made for this glorious consummation and not for any of those lesser ends in which fallen man is always tempted to acquiesce and indeed beyond which he is often unable to see. "Go, get thee to them of the captivity, unto the children of the people, and speak unto them and tell them, Thus saith the Lord God; whether they will hear or whether they will forbear."[2] This prophetic task of the Church, to declare the true nature of the world and of man, is one that is perennially incumbent upon her. But secondly, it is the

[1] *Sobornost'*, March 1937, p. 9.   [2] Ezekiel iii, 11.

Church's nature to be herself the redeemed community, the place in which, here and now, in spite of the sins and the blindness of her members, the sovereignty of God is manifested and the transformation of the world is anticipated. The Eucharistic rite, which is the source and centre of the Church's life, is both a symbol and a foretaste of the gathering of the human race into Christ and the transformation of the material world in him. The conversion of the bread and wine into the Body and Blood of Christ is the symbol and the foretaste of the transformation of the material world; the feeding of Christ's Body the Church with the Eucharistic gifts is the symbol and the foretaste of the gathering of the human race into Christ, for in communion, as St Augustine says, we *are* what we *receive*.[1] But here we must recall a truth which we considered in an earlier lecture, namely that, although from one aspect the Church is the ark of salvation in which the saved are protected from the flood outside, from another aspect the Church is not sealed off from the world at all, but is the source from which grace flows into the world to heal and transfigure it. Every time that the Eucharist is celebrated, the full, perfect and sufficient sacrifice, oblation and satisfaction which Christ offered throughout his life and on Calvary, and which is now a perpetually efficacious reality in the heavenly realm, is made a present and active power of redemption and sanctification in our world of space and time, and by their sharing

[1] Sermon, 227.

in it the members of Christ's Body the Church are sent out to their life in the world renewed and strengthened for their share in the work of the world's transformation. And now I will ask you to consider how the Church and the world are related in the civilisation in which we live.

There are times and places in which organised human society – the state – is explicitly governed by a view of human life which is plainly incompatible with the view of human life that is held by the Christian religion, and in which therefore the Church necessarily appears as either a socially subversive conspiracy or at least as a troublesome and obstructive influence: a permanent fly in the ointment, a recurrent spanner in the works. In such a society the Church is always liable to be persecuted, and the best it can hope for is a somewhat contemptuous toleration as long as it appears to be comparatively harmless; this is the condition in which the blood of the martyrs is the seed of the Church. It characterised the Church in the Roman Empire down to the time of Constantine; it characterised the Eastern Church from the Muslim conquest down to the collapse of the Turkish Empire in the present century; it characterises the Church in Russia and China today. It is a time of special glories, but also of special weaknesses; as Gregory Dix reminded us, there are failings, as well as virtues, to which a persecuted church is subject.[1] There are other times and places in which, with what-

[1] *The Shape of the Liturgy*, p. 388.

ever failings in practice, society explicitly accepts the
Christian view of God and man and organises itself
accordingly; the outstanding examples of this are, of
course, the Byzantine Empire and medieval Western
Christendom. The dangers to the Church in such a
situation are that it will either become to all intents and
purposes a department of the state or will set itself up
as a kind of super-state; the former danger menaced it in
Byzantium (and, we must honestly add, in post-
Reformation England), the latter in the medieval West,
though never, by the grace of God, totally. It is still
perhaps exemplified in Spain. In the modern world the
Church's situation is different from both of these, though
it partakes of the character of each. Furthermore, any
broad generalisation is impossible; what single description could accurately delineate the relation of the
Church to the social community in Ghana, India, the
United States, Germany, Indonesia and Great Britain?
However, if we except the countries behind the Iron
Curtain – and this is, of course, a very large exception
indeed – it is in general true to say that the Church today finds itself in what may be called a plural society,
that is to say a society in which there is no one generally
accepted doctrine about the end of man and the nature
of human life, but a general agreement to organise life
on a secularist basis, with welfare services provided by
the state and with as much toleration as possible for
the divergent views and interests of individuals. So far
as any underlying principle can be discerned it would

seem to be that of natural law and natural morality, and, whatever its limitations, this is not a principle that the Church can repudiate. Indeed its formulation has very largely been due to Christian thinkers, and it is noticeable that, while contemporary sociologists and jurists find it difficult to justify it theoretically, they seem to find it even more difficult to do without it. In most of Europe, and specially in Britain, the matter is complicated by the fact that there is, side by side with a determination not to let religion interfere with either public or private life, a widespread sentimental attachment to the forms of Christianity, as long as this is not taken as involving more than very occasional participation in public worship, and a vaguely benevolent feeling towards the Established Church. The average Englishman's or Scotsman's attitude to the Church seems to be that of keeping a rather reluctant hold of Nurse

for fear of finding something worse[1],

as appears from the recent survey which revealed that the large majority of unbelieving parents wish their children to receive Christian religious instruction in schools. I do not think, however, that we can count on this attitude continuing indefinitely. A state of affairs in which an almost total disregard of the Christian religion goes with a genuine good will towards the religious establishment seems to me to be too irrational

[1]. H. Belloc, *Cautionary Tales*, "Jim, Who ran away from his Nurse and was eaten by a Lion".

and unstable to endure. The condition of convinced and practising Christians in the modern world is, in fact, what Fr Karl Rahner has described by the Greek word *diaspora*, a "dispersion", "Christianity", he writes,

> exists *everywhere* in the world, and everywhere as a *diaspora*. It is effectually, *in terms of numbers*, a minority *everywhere*; nowhere does it fill such a role of effective leadership as would permit it to set upon the age with any force or clarity the stamp of a Christian ideal. Indeed, we are undoubtedly in an era which is going to see an increase in this *diaspora* character, no matter what causes we may assign to it.

But, Fr Rahner insists – and here I believe he is absolutely right – although we may, from an ideal standpoint, regret this state of affairs, we must also accept it as an inevitable "must" of the historic phase in which we live and in which we are called to exercise our Christian vocation. "For a believer", he continues,

> who judges things from God's standpoint, a "must" of this sort is not merely something with which he *may* reckon, but something with which he *must* reckon; something that he must calmly expect and at which he must not be surprised.[1]

Now in this *diaspora*-situation – this situation in which Christians are scattered among members of a non-

[1] *Mission and Grace*, I, "Christians in the Modern World", pp. 25, 28.

Christian or only nominally Christian society – the task of the Christian is a peculiarly double-sided one, a situation of mingled opportunity and peril. By his immersion in a non-Christian setting his own faith and morals are exposed to very strong and persistent stresses; it is therefore vitally necessary that he shall know just what his Christian allegiance commits him to as regards both belief and conduct, and he must also know why. On the other hand, just because he is not living in a ghetto but in the plural society he has repeated opportunities of influencing that society in a Christian direction. And here his position is extremely delicate, especially if he finds himself from time to time either in a Christian majority (for this can happen occasionally even in a plural society) or in a position in which he can make decisions binding on other people. For the question then arises as to how far he is entitled to impose his Christian standards on people who do not accept them and to whom they may well appear irrational or tyrannical. It is not enough simply to say that he must not try to get them accepted. He does not cease to be a citizen because he is a Christian; and one of the duties of a citizen is to encourage society to live in accordance with the standards that he believes to be socially healthy, and for him these will be Christian standards. Other people will try to get their schemes of values embodied in practice; it is equally a duty and a right that he should try to get his. On the other hand, he must recognise that to force upon others standards which they conscientiously repudiate is to overrule their responsibility and their rights as free men and women and can only produce exasperation and resentment. At the present time we see this problem arising in such realms as those of marriage and sexual matters in general, of penal practice and of religious education. There can be no simple answer as regards Christian policy in such a situation, and the matter is complicated by the fact that on matters of detail, as contrasted with general principles, Christians may not be in entire agreement with one another. Thus, together with a firm and intelligent grasp of our own faith and a disciplined living of the Christian life we must combine a sensitive and sympathic approach to others and a genuine readiness to enter into their understanding and outlook. As Rahner says, "if our presentation of Christian principles is to be effective, then what applies to the winning of an individual must apply also to our public presentation of ideas amongst the masses; we must begin with the things for which we can expect some understanding, and go on slowly step by step."[1] And in particular we must avoid any appearance of self-righteousness, of suggesting that it is as a reward of our own merits or as a consequence of our own superior intelligence that we have been given the faith that we profess, and not by the sheer mercy of God. Rather we should apply to ourselves the reply which Père Charles gave to the question why the Gospel had been brought

[1] ibid., p. 46.

to the peoples of Europe so many centuries before those of Asia and Africa, that when you are shovelling away a pile of muck you begin at the bottom. But, above all, we must make it plain, both in our talk and still more in the quality of our living, that the Christian lives in a larger, richer and more interesting world than that of the secularist, a world of constant and delightful surprises, that he has access to sources of strength of which the secularist is ignorant, even when by the grace of God they are bringing forth in the secularist's own life fruits whose origin he cannot recognise, and beyond all this, that the Christian can use disappointment, frustration and agony in such a way that they become redemptive and creative. We must make it plain, too, that, while our perspective is not limited by the death of our bodies but extends beyond the grave into an eternity of union with God, we are nevertheless not uninterested in this world and its concerns but on the contrary look forward to its transformation into the glory of the risen Christ and see our concern with it while we are in this life as being our share in this work of transfiguration.

The Christian, then, faced with the challenge of a secularist age, is neither to repudiate the secular nor to capitulate to it; he is to claim it for God and enter into its life in order to play his part in making that claim good. "The transfiguration of the secular", "The supernaturalisation of the natural" – it is in such phrases as these that I would sum up the Church's task in this, as in every age. Clearly there is no question of loosening our grip upon the supernatural realities in order to enter more fully into the concerns of secular man; quite the opposite. It is only by tightening our hold on the super- natural that we can enter into the secular order with any hope of transforming it and without being swamped and drowned by it. We need more frequent and regular participation in the Eucharist and more frequent and regular reception of Christ's Body and Blood; we need more costing confessions and more eagerly welcomed absolutions. And most of all we need prayer. For most people today, prayer is both more necessary and more difficult than ever before. The traditional methods of prayer were largely devised for people who had more time and less distractions than most of us have today, and they seem of very little use to present-day people. I cannot attempt to go into detail about this in the few minutes that still remain to me. I would only remark that for most people today prayer needs to be very simple, very direct, very natural, a matter of looking at God and loving him rather than of addressing elaborate speeches to him, a matter of letting him act upon us rather than of giving our good advice to him, and, while it is absolutely essential that we should find times, how- ever brief, which are devoted to prayer and nothing else, it is no less essential that our prayer shall, as it were, soak through and permeate our life as a whole, so that all our activity and the setting in which it takes place, shall be part of our prayer-offering to God, even those activities in which it would be impossible, or indeed sometimes positively wrong, for us to be consciously thinking about him.

Again, because we are all one in Christ's body the Church, we shall see our own prayer and activity as simply part of the prayer and activity of the whole body and therefore as taken up into the prayer and activity of Christ himself. And this will give us the greatest encouragement in those times when our own prayer is dry and dull and our own activity apparently frustrated and unfruitful, the times when, in one way or another, we feel really "up against it"; our little effort is part of something infinitely bigger than itself and it is taken up into the greater reality. (For a thoroughly realistic discussion of the place and method of Christian prayer in the conditions of modern life I should like to recommend to you Sister Edna Mary's excellent little book *This World and Prayer*; I do not think it could be bettered.) And it is in this context of the whole Body that we should see the central place in the Church's strategy that is held by those religious communities which are specially dedicated to the life of prayer; it is in them that the Church's real warfare is being fought, on that deep level of being where Michael and his angels fight against the dragon and his angels, for this kind goeth not out save by prayer and fasting. And it is through them more than through any other channel, that there flows into the world the power for its regeneration and transfiguration.

As I said at the beginning of this lecture, there are any number of live issues with which Christians are faced today about which, for lack of time or ability or both, I have said little or nothing. I have said nothing about war, nothing about sex, nothing about the race problem, the population explosion, demythologising, Christian reunion, existentialism or logical analysis. Neither Hebrew scrolls nor computers have received so much as a mention. But I have tried to say something about God and the world and man and the Church and our task in the contemporary situation. In conclusion I should like to plead that we shall not allow the particular difficulties of the present day to throw us off our balance or to distort our perspective. And I should like to end with some more sentences from Fr Karl Rahner, who is, I venture to think, one of the greatest, if not always one of the easiest to read, of the theologians of our time.

An apostolate on the offensive, not exhausting itself in desperate efforts to save what is beyond salvage (the Church considered *as identical* with everybody in a given area), need have no fear of being fruitless in the long run. The apparent atrophy of the religious sense today is a passing phenomenon; in the period of vast upheaval in which we live, of which the past century of industrialism is only the beginning, it was, *in concreto*, absolutely unavoidable and to be expected. . . . Man's religious sense is ineradicable, nor can it, in the long run, be appeased by pseudo-objects provided by secular utopianism, economic, social or cultural. . . .

Of course, for all this we need faith in eternal life; a faith so strong that it is ready to purchase eternal life by the witness of earthly death. We are often lacking in this uncompromising faith. . . . But in the *diaspora* situation, only he can endure to the end who truly believes in eternal life and in the promises of God.[1]

[1] ibid., pp. 53f.